ALMOST LOST

The True Story of an Anonymous Teenager's Life on the Streets

edited by
BEATRICE SPARKS, Ph.D

AN AVON FLARE BOOK

This is a work of nonfiction based on the actual counseling sessions between Dr. Sparks and a suicidal teenager. Names and places have been changed at the request of "Sammy's" parents.

AVON BOOKS, INC.
1350 Avenue of the Americas
New York, New York 10019

Copyright © 1996 by Beatrice M. Sparks
Published by arrangement with the editor
Library of Congress Catalog Card Number:96-2457
ISBN: 0-380-78341-X
RL: 7.0
www.avonbooks.com

Library of Congress Cataloging in Publication Data:
Almost lost : the true story of an anonymous teenager's life on the
    streets / edited by Beatrice Sparks.
       p.   cm.
         1. Depression in adolescence—Treatment—Case studies—Juvenile literature. 2. Adolescent psychotherapy—Case studies—Juvenile literature. 3. Family psychotherapy—Case studies—Juvenile literature. I. Sparks, Beatrice.
RJ506.D4A46   1996   96-2457
616.85'2706'0835—dc20   CIP
                                                              AC

First Avon Flare Printing: June 1996

AVON FLARE TRADEMARK REG. U.S. PAT. OFF. AND IN OTHER COUNTRIES, MARCA REGISTRADA, HECHO EN U.S.A.

Printed in the U.S.A.

To Sammy

Thank you Sammy for not blowing out your candle. You light up the universe for all of us who know you, as well as lighting up the lives of those who will read about your experiences.

People do not die from suicide; they die from sadness.

Anonymous

FOREWORD

Traveling with Sammy on his real-life therapeutic road to recovery allows parents, teachers, friends, etc., to see what they may be doing that is right; or what they may be doing literally to foster dangerous, perhaps even suicidal, behavior in someone, including themselves.

Sammy, with his parents' approval, has consented to help others through the "scary, black, pain-filled, unbelonging no-way-out nothingness" that he has recently exited by allowing his edited therapy session tapes to be assembled into the book *Almost Lost*.

Love ya, Sammy.

Dr. Phillip Morgenstern
Family Guidance Service Director

Sammy knows me but he doesn't know that in the past I've tried to "off" myself too. I didn't know any ways out then. BUT I DO NOW! THANKS SAMMY!

P.J.

I always thought I had to be perfect. Sometimes it was so hard I contemplated suicide. Now I know people, even my mother and father, should accept and respect me as imperfect as I sometimes am. That knowledge is a great relief.

Name withheld at request

I've wondered what it would be like to go through therapy. I thought it would be deep and scary, like someone getting you to remember things that were horrible and maybe didn't even happen. Now I know it's more like looking for the good stuff, and I wish that my whole family could learn to listen and play help-yourself and everybody else head games and learn to get along more, and help each of us get rid of the bad hurting stuff in our lives, like Sammy and his family did.

Marianne, age 14

My family has lots of problems. There's no way we could afford a psychologist, though, for counseling. I've gone to the school counselor, but she's got so many sent to her she can't even remember our names. I'm going to try to get my family to read this book together. It can't hurt—but helping? I guess I can be positive and hope. We need lots of help, though.

Josh, age 16

ALMOST LOST

Paula Gordon, Registered Nurse, called regarding therapy for her son, Samuel Gordon, age 15

SYMPTOMS

Samuel has gone from being a bright, happy, funny, usually self-confident boy to someone who often seems "almost an old senile stranger."

1. His mother notices a continuing loss of self-esteem.

2. Difficulty in concentration and/or remembering.

3. Unusual irritability.

4. Spurts of, for no apparent reason, blatant hostility.

5. Appetite loss. On rare occasions, gorging.

6. Melancholy periods that come oftener, stay longer.

7. Times when he locks himself in his room and she can hear him crying pitifully.

8. He seems to feel completely detached from everyone and everything.

9. His grades have fallen from As and Bs to Ds and Fs.

10. He has quit his part-time job.

Samuel Gordon Chart
Monday, April 4, 2:00 P.M.
———————

Edited tape from first visit
SAMUEL (SAMMY) GORDON, 15 years old

"Hi, Samuel. I'm Doctor B."

"Hi." Samuel sounded as depleted as if he had just done his best, but still finished dead last, in an exhausting marathon that he had really wanted to win.

"Do you like to be called Samuel, Sam, Sammy, or something else?"

He shrugged.

"I want you to know that anything you say in this session is completely between the two of us. I am required by law to keep it confidential. I am even more bound by my own code of ethics to honor and respect your thoughts and concepts and words absolutely."

Samuel continues. "What I really want is for you and the rest of the whole screwed-up world, including me, to just quickly and quietly dissolve into nothing, never-was, nothingness."

"You don't know me but . . ."

"I kind of know you through your books."

"I hope you know how much I cared for each of *those kids*."

"I guess."

"Do you think I would care less about you?"

He shrugged.

"I want to be completely honest with you so that

you can feel safe in being straightforward and honest with me—that is, if you want to be. Does that sound fair?"

"Ummm . . ."

"If I feel someone I talk with is an endangerment to himself or herself, or to others, I might on a rare occasion feel it necessary to seek help beyond my own ability, but *only* in a professional way. I hope that makes sense to you."

"It doesn't. Why can't everybody just live, or not live, their own life?"

"Because sometimes people can't see their glorious future through their glucky present."

"That's Establishment horse hockey."

"Your mom told me that you didn't want to come, didn't think you needed to come."

"For once the warden and keeper was right."

"Did you have any particular reason for *not* wanting to see me?"

"Why would anyone in their right mind *wanna* see a shrink?"

"What's the difference between seeing a medical doctor when you suffer from physical pain and seeing a therapist when you're hurting mentally? Isn't the pain you have now as real as any pain could be?"

"It's not really pain. It's . . ."

"You mean it's not like a broken leg."

"Yeah."

"But it's still deep, dark, cold discomfort isn't it?"

(Deep sigh.) "Sometimes even my hair hurts."

"Would you like to talk about what is hurting you?"

"No."

"Would it help to try to find out why you're sad?"

"Uh-huh."

Samuel pulled into himself like a turtle pulling into its shell.

"Would you like to feel better? Like your old, old, olden self?"

"I almost don't even remember that person."

"But would you like to go back again to a happy, uncluttered, unpressured existence?"

"I'm not sure I *ever was* that way."

"Do you think maybe you're depressed?"

"No way! My mom probably gave you a bunch of gobbly goop poop about that. Actually, she has not clue one. What she's really looking for is *absolute, complete remote control of my life.*"

"You think she wants to *completely control* your life?"

"Seems like it."

"How does that make you feel?"

"Like hell. Makes me wanna get the hell outta there and off the planet."

"Does your mom know that?"

"She should. I've told her often enough."

"Think about this question for a minute. Maybe your mom's pushy, but do you think she tries to give you suggestions and guidelines and boundaries because she *hates you* or because *she loves you?*"

"Who knows?"

"You honestly don't know?"

"I honestly don't care."

"Did you know that depression is a lot more than just a long downer? It's loneliness, apathy, loss of interest and pleasure and curiosity. I wish you'd talk with me about depression even if *you* don't have it. Lots of kids do, you know. In fact, it is estimated that over eighteen million people today suffer from depression, *many, many of them kids!*"

"Eighteen million?"

"The sad thing is that lots of depression goes undiagnosed and untreated because people don't want to accept the symptoms for what they are. They don't know that it *can* be diagnosed and treated. Anyone who is going through a state of unhappiness or nonfeeling deserves to know that it is practically always temporary and that he or she is *not alone!* Not the *only person* in the entire universe who feels that way, but just *one* out of eighteen million."

"I thought I was the only one so sort of unhinged and out of touch."

"Believe me, you're not! I'd say that most kids go through some degree of depression, at one point or another before they become adults. And they're usually pretty good at covering it up. There are probably many kids *you know* who, to one degree or another, feel much as you do, *right now!*"

"Ohhh no."

"Ohh yes."

"You've got statistics and studies and stuff."

"I certainly have. Would you like to talk about them?"

"Umm . . ."

"Perhaps I can show you how to shuffle things around a little in your life so *you* can let some extra sunshine and happiness in if you want to do that. I can't *make* you change. Your mom can't make you change, your dad can't, but—"

Samuel clapped his hands over his ears. "I don't want to talk about *him!* I *won't* talk about *him!*"

"Is it possible then that he is the very one we should be talking about?

"*No way! No way!* He doesn't exist. He never did. He's less than nothing in my life, and I'm less than

nothing in his. He's just blank space. Forget him . . .
erase him . . . rub him out.''

"Okay, relax. We can do that. You are sure,
though, that talking about him won't ease the pressure and the anger and the hurt that you're feeling
right now?''

I could sense that the tiny thread of hope and rap-
port that had barely started to build between us
was unraveling.

"I don't want to talk about *him* or anything. I
don't want to feel anything, taste anything . . . or
anything. I just want to . . . pull the plug . . . do the
deed . . . get it over with. It's my candle. I should
be able to blow it out if I want to.''

"You're talking about suicide? We can talk
about suicide.''

"I *don't!* I *won't* talk about suicide! I can't even
do *IT* right. They make it sound so easy on the tapes,
so peaceful, so out-of-it, so what I want. The lyrics
'just dying to die' run around in my brain day and
night like a squirrel in a cage. I can't stop it.''

"You can if you allow someone to teach you how.
Try sloooowing dooooown, sloow doown . . . slow
down. Take some big, deep, slow breaths. Now quietly and slowly let *one* little beam of sunlight float
softly into your brain.''

"I don't want to! I like it here inside myself,
where I'm protected, where it's all mushy and
squished together and quicksandy tarrish black. I'm
up to my neck in the goo . . . almost gone . . .''

Samuel closed his eyes and relaxed. The lines
melted from his face and the faintest of smiles took
over. It was as if he was in the deepest of self-
imposed trances.

"I'm almost a forever part of the forever black

nothingness that forever floats slowly between the planets in the black galaxy, through black infinity . . . just waiting for my mouth and nose to be sucked under and filled up.''

"Have you thought about the pain that would be felt by your loved ones who would be left behind?"

Tears started streaming down Samuel's face and his nose ran.

"I want them to feel it! I want my dad to feel it in every nerve and muscle and bone and pore of his body. I want him to feel it a million, trillion, zillion times more than I do, if that's possible."

"What about your mom? Would it make you feel good to have her feel that sad and bad?"

"No! No way do I want her to be hurt."

Samuel clammed up so tightly I could see it would be prudent to change subjects, at least temporarily.

"Do you know much about hypnosis?"

"No."

"I saw by one momentary spark in your eyes that you know something."

"I saw a guy at the high school one time make kids think they were chickens and stuff."

"Did you find that interesting?"

"Maybe so at that time and place."

"Would you like to know more about hypnosis?"

"Why? I told you I'm outta here as soon as I can get my hands on . . ." He stopped.

"Wouldn't you, just in the slightest curious way, like me to show you how to use hypnosis positively instead of negatively as it was used when you saw it demonstrated?"

"You mean like you put *me* in a trance and make me think I'm a pig or an insane person or something?"

"No, no, no. I mean if you want me to, I'll show

7

you how to put yourself in a trance so that you can remember some of the happy things in your past life, or see the good fun possibilities for your future. You will like it, I promise.''

"I don't think so.''

"Aw, come on. Let's try.''

"No.''

"Doesn't one single moment of your childhood that was happy or funny or filled with sunshine flicker through your mind ever?''

"No.''

"Do you mean you can't remember or you choose not to remember?''

"I dunno. My mind doesn't seem to be working, and, besides, I don't care. Nothing would be worth remembering, even if I could remember it, or wanted to, or had the energy to.''

"What have you got to lose?''

"Not much. Besides, nothing could be much more boring than this.''

"Gee, thanks.''

Sullen grunt with tiniest hint of an embarrassed grin behind it.

"Let me introduce you to hypnosis as it was meant to be practiced, actually has been practiced, for thousands of years: for relaxation, for focusing, for peace and comfort, for healing and for concentration. Did you know that hypnosis is used by many athletes who want to control their bodies more efficiently, and by people who want to focus better or pass their bar exams—all sorts of things. It's also used to control pain and/or to help people fill up the emptiness that, on occasion, may come into their lives.''

"Can it really control pain and stuff like that?''

"Absolutely! It can also bring reality back into focus if a person gives it a chance."

"Well ..."

"Are you ready?"

Samuel looked *at* me, not through me, for the first time, thought for a moment, then got to his feet and shuffled out.

"First I gotta go to the bathroom."

SUMMARY OF SESSION

Samuel did not return from the men's room.

He is in a major depressive state, in a mode where he could easily endanger himself.

I am deeply concerned about him. Although I know it is unprofessional, I sense that I am somehow blaming myself for what I should have done, might have done, etc. Hopefully, Samuel will think things over and come back—*soon*.

Five Days Later
Paula Gordon Chart
Friday, April 8, 9:35 A.M.

Paula Gordon phoned. Samuel has disappeared. She is distraught.

Friday, April 8, 4:30 P.M.

First Visit
PAULA GORDON, *mother of Samuel Gordon*

"I'm Paula Gordon, Sammy's mother. I'm worried crazy to death about him. He hasn't been home for five days. I can't eat, I can't sleep, I can't think. In fact, I'm afraid that I might accidentally do something to endanger a patient."

"Relax. It's normal for you to be worried. That is a part of being a loving, caring mother."

"But I'm such a bad mother, always waffling, being too strict or too permissive, never being absolutely positive about anything I do regarding him. I'm sure that many of Sammy's problems are my fault. For the last few months I've been so fearful of offending him or demeaning him or lowering his already-low self-esteem that ... it's like I'm almost *afraid* of him. Is it possible to be afraid of your own son?"

"None of the above is as important as, 'Do you love him?' That's Number 1."

"I love him with a kind of love I didn't even know was possible until I became pregnant. I loved him when he was just a microscopic fertilized egg. Lance and I talked to him and called him Eggbert. Even before we were married we planned on having him. We both came from broken homes and we wanted our baby to have a perfect existence."

"Do you think anyone has a *perfect* existence?"

"Maybe not, but I knew then, and I know now, so little about mothering. If I'd just known more, maybe I could have done better."

"Do you have other children?"

"Two daughters, ten and thirteen."

"How are they doing?"

"Great. Sometimes it's like they are a different species than Sammy."

"How?"

"I don't know. I certainly didn't mean it the way it came out."

"What is one of the differences?"

"Well . . . on rare occasions I have to work longer hours if the hospital is short-handed or I pull an extra shift or two if there are emergencies. I'm not home enough. It seems I'm never there when Sammy wants me or needs to talk."

"Does he talk to you and tell you his needs when you are there?"

"Well, no. It's more and more like he shuts himself up inside himself and I can't get through. Besides, when we do talk, I always seem to say the wrong thing at the wrong time, in the wrong way."

"Can you talk with your daughters agreeably, at least most of the time?"

"Yes, most of the time we pretty much understand each other."

"Are you a good nurse?"

"Of course I am. Why do you ask?"

"Because you said you were a bad mother. Are you really a bad mother?"

"I honestly don't know. Dana and Dorie say I'm not, but sometimes I get mad and let it show . . . or close up to keep from cracking up . . . or go in the bathroom, turn the water on and cry my heart out. Most of the time now I feel *so* frustrated . . . and helpless and hopeless and ineffective and unnurturing. I can't seem to get through to Sammy and . . . sadly I've found that even love is not enough . . . and money is not enough. I went through a stage where I tried to buy him everything and it didn't work. And I've prayed and I've prayed and I've prayed . . . and I've failed and I've failed and I've failed. I want so much for him to be happy and fulfilled and outgoing and all the wonderful things he

11

used to be but ... I can't seem to make him do any of the things that would bring him joy.''

"That is a sad truism."

"What?"

"That you can't *make* him do anything. All human beings are born with free agency, and it seems very easy for some to *choose negative paths which can only lead to negative destinations!*"

"But I can't just give up on him. I won't!"

"You're right! You must *never* give up on him, but you can stop beating up on yourself for not being perfect. No one is perfect. *Try loving yourself as much as you love him.*"

"But I want, I need, *him* to love *me!* He doesn't think I love him or that I care, or understand, or empathize, or want him to be *him.* And it seems that no matter how hard I try, he doesn't ... well ... like me. Often I think he can't stand me! He has no respect for me." (Her anguish was almost physical.)

"Shhh. Relax and think about what I'm going to say seriously and calmly for a moment. *How do you think Sammy can possibly like or respect you, when at this point he doesn't like or respect himself? People who are going through a depressed or angry time in their lives see everything and everyone in direct ratio to how they see themselves.* Does that make sense to you?"

"A little. I know he's suffering deeply, and I know it doesn't help him or me, but I'm suffering along with him."

"You're a good woman! And a great mom!"

"No, no, no."

"Yes, yes, yes. And Sammy does love you. You are his anchor, his foundation."

"I know your sessions with people are confidential, but did he say that? Did he actually say that?"

"Yes, he said it. Not verbally but nonverbally in many, many ways."

"That makes me feel a little better. I guess as long as he knows I love him, and I know he loves me, maybe we will survive through this stage of his growth process. It *is* just a stage isn't it?"

"In most cases, lost kids do find themselves."

"Oh, thank you, thank you, thank you *for telling me that!* I've been so scared, and I've tried so hard to be a good mother, but obviously I haven't made it." She hunched in her chair. "I did try though, to do my best."

"I believe you, and if you've done the best you know how, be comforted. Let peace rest in your heart and mind. YOUR BEST *IS* GOOD ENOUGH."

"Actually, I'm not honestly sure I've ever really, truly done my . . . very best."

"Don't waste energy on that. In all my years as a therapist I've never met one single woman who felt she had done an adequate job as a mother—had felt totally satisfied with her every attitude and action—and that certainly includes me. We've all read about Abraham Lincoln and others who talked about their 'angel mothers' who never raised their voices, or got short-tempered, or felt 'put upon,' etc. I suspect most of those memories *were much more nostalgic than accurate*. So don't worry about getting impatient or frustrated, or even raising your voice and ragging once in a while. Those things often show how *much* you care."

"I *do* care."

"Then raise your mind-set to a level where it's positive and optimistic, for *pessimism and negativism are both literally powerful toxins.* They can poison your mind and body as surely as any lethal chemical. Pessimism and negativism are both *forms of self-abuse!''*

"I'd never thought about that before, but it makes sense. I'm going to start working on putting more positive, optimistic concepts into my life."

"When?"

"Right away."

"What about *right now?''*

"Okay, *right now!''*

"If you'd like, I'll give you a positive relaxation exercise. It's an autogenic type of training that can help you lessen your anxiety, stress, and tension—a form of self-hypnosis which can help you to help yourself both physically and mentally."

"I can use that."

My voice slowed down and became softer: (The following is a condensed version of a twenty-minute introduction to hypnotherapy.)

"See that tiny little dark spot on the ceiling. You might want to stare at it. Relax ... stare at it ... concentrate only on that one small spot. Your eyes may be getting heavy and hard to hold open. If you wish, close them and nestle down snugly into your chair, your head resting comfortably on the back. Invite your unconscious mind to pass soothing messages to your relaxing body."

My voice slowed even more until *each word* seemed fluidly elongated. I repeated each phrase three times.

"I feel quite quiet ... quite quiet ... quite quiet ...

"I am relaxing easily ... relaxing easily ... relaxing easily ...

"Breathing slowly and deeply ... slowly and deeply ... slowly and deeply ...

"My right arm feels heavy ... feels heavy ... feels heavy ...

"My left arm feels heavy ... feels heavy ... feels heavy ...

"My neck and shoulder muscles feel unstrained and relaxed ... unstrained and relaxed ... unstrained and relaxed ...

"My right leg feels heavy ... feels heavy ... feels heavy ...

"My left leg feels heavy ... feels heavy ... feels heavy ...

"I am feeling quietly relaxed ... quietly relaxed ... all over ...

"I feel my self-control levels slowly, warmly, and comfortingly, increasing in every molecule of my body and mind ... I feel my self-control levels slowly, warmly, and comfortingly, increasing in every molecule of my body and mind.

"You may want to take a few seconds to move the muscles in your shoulders and neck and hands and feet slowly before you open your eyes."

"Ohhhh, that was soooo nice. I wish you could relax me like that many times a day."

"I can't, but *you* can! I am going to give you, as you leave, a complete copy of the SET NUMBER 1 concept that you've just experienced. You'll probably want to silently in your subconscious repeat and comply with each phrase at least twice a day, in a quiet, thoughtful way. You'll find that the more often you return your body to a state of restful quiet, the higher your energy and self-control will be when you start working again.

"Oops! I almost forgot to ask you to tell me something about Sammy's father."

"There's not much to tell. I helped Lance through

school till he became a computer programmer in Silicon Valley, then he decided we were not 'with it' enough and unceremoniously dumped us. It's okay though. He regularly sends money for the kids, and I bought our nice home with the divorce settlement money. I don't really think there's much stress in our lives connected with him anymore."

"What about his relationship with Sammy?"

"Since the divorce he hasn't been a great part of the girls' lives, but Sammy has visited him on Christmas holidays and school breaks."

"You didn't sense anything different in Sammy's behavior after his last visit?"

"I don't think so, but while Sammy was gone, Lance's aunt, who was visiting us, fell and fractured her femur. I guess I was pretty busy with her. Should I have noticed something?"

"Not necessarily. For now just quit worrying so much about your kids and *start taking a little more interest in the hurting little child within yourself.* She needs love and attention, too, you know."

"It seems like there's not much energy left for *me* these days. I'm so concerned about Sammy. He's on my mind day and night, morning and afternoon."

"Does that interfere with your work or your relationship with your daughters, do you think?"

"Possibly ... probably! But I don't seem able to control the sometimes stabbing, almost-suffocating fears I have regarding my *boy,* who has become almost a stranger to me. I guess what I'm really trying to say is I feel constantly guilty because ..." She shrugged.

"Are you saying that you're allowing your fears and negative positionings to take over and *control* your life in a sense?"

"I'm afraid so."

"Are there physical ways in which your stressors are manifesting themselves?"

"Oh, yes. I, who seldom had headaches, now not only have them in my head but also in my neck. If one can have headaches in her neck. Anyway, it's the same indescribable black-iron pulsing pressure. I'm ashamed to admit that one day I hurt so much I actually found myself crouched in a fetal position in a corner of my closet, rocking back and forth. It was frightening. In fact, I think that was the incident that convinced me to come see you."

"You truly need relief from your troubling emotions and pain, don't you?"

"Yes, but I'm desperately afraid of becoming dependent on meds. You wouldn't believe the number of women I see and know who are hooked on prescription stuff."

"Yes I would but let's not worry about that. For the moment we're only interested in *you*. Would you like to try a simple but effective mind-over-matter exercise? I think you will respond very well to the procedure."

"At this point I'm ready to do anything to alleviate the stress and the pain."

"At this moment, what rating would you give your discomforting feelings?"

"Rating, like in numbers?"

"Yes."

"You mean 1 to 10?"

"I mean 1 to whatever number you feel good with."

"Well, I guess *all together* today, it's about a thirty."

"Close your eyes, loosen your tight, tense mus-

17

cles. Let peace flow over you in a soft white film. See your number thirty in big red neon figures.''

"I can see it.''

"Can you see it clearly?''

"Yes.''

"Then slowly and carefully will it away from you. Watch it drift farther and farther away for about ten seconds to a minute. I'll talk you through the exercise this time and when you get home you can allow your unconscious to repeat the process if, or as, needed.''

My voice slowed down and became softer.

"First relax. Quietly, soothingly, peacefully relax. Start with the hair follicles on the top of your head ... slowly ... slowly ... relax them. Relax down the sides of your face, which is becoming smoother and smoother ... past your ears ... your eyes ... your nose.''

As I talked I occasionally reached out and softly touched a part of her body as I referred to it.

"Your face is now totally unlined and relaxed. Your head and neck pains are noticeably lessening. They are fading ... bleaching ... softening from metal-hard black, tight and taut, to a soft, more pliable, light grey color. You have rated your discomfort at 30—the number is drifting away from you ... from a squeezing, metallic tense 30 to a softer, less imprisoning 29 ... 28 ... 27. Watch the discomfort ball being pulled farther and farther away by some unseen force. Relax your hands ... relax your arms ... relax your shoulders. Your tension is drifting out ... 26 ... 25 ... 24. As your upper and lower torso relax, your breathing slows down, your head and neck feelings become, not painful but interesting ... 23 ... 22 ... 21 ... 19. Negative feelings are detaching from your body as you relax your lower back and hips ... 18 ... 17 ... 16. As you relax your thighs and legs the numbers drift still farther away ... 15 ... 14 ... 13. When you completely relax your ankles and feet, your whole body detaches from discomfort and negativeness ... 12 ... 11 ... 10 ... 9 ... all badness is floating far away from your body. Your toes and the soles of your feet feel warm and comfortable ... 8 ... 7 ... 6 ... 5. All the muscles, nerves, fibers in your body are relaxed, soft, white, pliable ... 4 ... 3 ... 2 ... 1.

"You feel good, secure, comfortable, relaxed, and confident. Thank yourself gently for allowing these sacred, warm, belonging feelings to exist within you. Imprint upon your mind the fact that *good feelings are like music: the more you practice, the more skilled you become at doing what you want to do, becoming what you want to become, feeling what you want to feel, and thinking what you want to think.* Remind yourself to notice those positive feelings and welcome them.

"As you slowly approach a perfect body-relaxed state you see your complete package of discomforts disappearing over the horizon. Take three big, big, big breaths. Yawn and jiggle all the parts of your body like your kids used to do when they were little and played 'rubber man' or 'Jell-O person.' Remind yourself that life is wonderful, intriguing, exciting, and that you are willing on occasion, to struggle through a cold, hard, dark, painful, sometimes frightening, valley to get to the sunny, protective, love-filled hill that lies on the other side. Stretch and flex your muscles. Smile. Open your eyes. How do you feel?"

"Great."

"What is your discomfort ratio?"

"Wow! I forgot about it."

"Want it back?"

"No, thank you."

"If it does creep up on you again, do you think you can handle the procedure we've just practiced?"

"By myself?"

"No. With your *subconscious mind helping your conscious.* That is what hypnotherapy is all about when it's used properly, which means positively!"

"I think ..."

"You think?"

"No. I *know* I can do it! I must! For my girls and my job and my sanity as well as for Sammy. Now, how can I handle the fearful overwhelming thoughts that clutch and claw at me during a lot of torturous, endless black nights?"

"You can practice the two soothing, relaxing, control exercises I've given you. Sometimes we think of *control* as being an imprisoning, inflexible, concrete thing when actually it's a part of love's lifting, releasing-from-bondage process. The kind of *control* we want is the kind that puts *you* in charge, makes *you* the master instead of the slave."

"That is interesting. I'd never thought of *control* as being a friendly kind of word before."

"Sometimes you may have to get up out of your warm, soft bed and exercise vigorously to prove to yourself that *you control* your body as well as your mind! Tell yourself, 'MOVE OUT LEGS, MOVE OUT ARMS, MOVE UP LEGS, MOVE UP ARMS, ETC.,' and whatever you do, don't let the unseen, unreal NIGHT BOGIES get to you till they *control you.* I suspect most people on earth have, at one time or another, had the tormenting NIGHT BOGIES creep around in their heads, trying to nibble away their brains. Have you ever heard the old spiritual

'Lord, You Made the Nights Too Long'? Most of us have been visited by the bogies during a death, an illness, a divorce, or one of the thousands of other debilitating traumas, like the one you are now suffering through with Sammy. You are *not* alone.''

''It's reassuring to know *I'm not alone*. In some selfish, strange way I haven't been thinking about anybody else's problems at all. The starving children in Africa, the people existing in war-torn Bosnia, the Haitians in their leaky boats, the differing kinds of horrendous abuses in our own country—all seemed unimportant, as well as the problems of other moms with wayward, somewhat rebellious sons and daughters. They barely existed until now—only me ... selfish, wanting everything my way, self-centered me.''

I laughed. ''I hate to break up your 'pretty, potent, petty, pity party' as one kid called hers after she got her life back on track, but remember that *negative thinking or talking or doing to or about yourself or anyone else is a form of permanently maiming abuse.*''

''Oops, I forgot.''

''That's okay. We all get a little maudlin once in a while, so forget it. Just think about the assignment you're going to give yourself to get *your* life in order so that *you* can more effectively help Sammy do the same for his, when he gets to the place where he wants and will accept your help.''

''Well, first I've got to keep reminding myself that *I am not alone!* I am not the only one in the world trying to solve major as well as minor problems.''

''And ...''

''I've got to rely more on *my* control of myself.''

''How?''

"Through relaxation and positive thinking and not spending so much time dwelling on the worst possible outcome for every *occasion, particularly as it applies to Sammy.*"

"Another thing you might want to consider adding to your new pile of tricks, Paula, is the concept of *learning to be as nice to YOURSELF as you would like to have others be to you.* Have you heard the saying from the Bible, 'Do unto others as you would have them do unto you'?"

"Yes."

"Don't you think that also means, 'DO UNTO *YOURSELF* AS YOU WOULD *HAVE* OTHERS DO UNTO YOU'?"

Paula thought for a while. "It probably does, but I . . ."

"You what?"

"I don't know . . ."

"You mean you don't know where to start?"

"I guess."

"Want me to help you?"

"It sounds really simple, and I sense it would work but I . . . yes, please, please help me. I'm trying hard not to, but I feel sooooo inadequate."

"Have you ever *put yourself first?*"

"Put myself first? I hope not! Not since I had kids, anyway. They are my life, my main reason for living. I'm certainly not going to *allow* them to go through what I went through all my growing-up years."

"Have you ever considered what might happen to them if you *allow yourself,* through neglect of *your* mental and physical health, to become impaired or incapacitated? You've mentioned that your concentration and interest in things have diminished, and that each day you are feeling more tired and unenthusiastic."

"That thought is frightening. I won't let anything happen to me. I can't!"

"Would you like to listen to an explanation of our *SOMETIMES ME FIRST PROGRAM?* You'll be surprised to find out that it's anything but a selfish, 'I want mine first-bigger-better-more costly and luxurious than anyone else's type program. It's really a humble, 'I must take good care of myself mentally and physically and spiritually to help other people make the most of themselves in those areas' program. A Mental Health Sometimes Me First concept is the exact opposite of a selfish, self-centered one. You'll like it."

"I like everything you've taught me, and it makes sense that first I have to learn how to swim before I can keep my kids and the other people I love afloat. But you've presented so many get-me-out-of-my-black-hole, exciting things in this first session, I'm not sure I can remember them all."

"That's the reason we're making a tape. You can take it home and listen as many times as you want and make notes if you'd like or, if there is anything too personal or that might be painful to yourself or others, feel free to come back here to check out your tape and go over it in our little private Listening Room. It used to be a storage area, but now it's a cozy place for *you* to listen again to *yourself* as well as to me."

"Be sure I will *use it!* On my lunch hours if that's okay."

"You might want to call before you come to see if the Listening Room is in use, or to make a reservation. I'm sure you'll find rehearing and contemplating

23

what we've said on your tape will be an added support system—and at no extra cost."

"When I came here I had no idea I was going to go home trying to work on *myself* and *my new positive attitude.*"

"That is an important concept! Most people don't realize how *contagious* attitudes are; negative ones can flit through a home, an office, a school, a community, faster than measles, the flu, or even the common cold, often with very serious and possibly *permanent* repercussions."

"I can't wait to get home and start using *positive* therapy on Dana and Dorie. And soon, oh, I do hope soon, on Sammy. I know he will come home, and I *can* wait a while. When I came in here I thought I couldn't, but I *can* and I *will.*"

SUMMARY OF SESSION

Paula Gordon's pain has been somewhat relieved. She has been given three concepts to work on: 1. Set 1-Relaxation; 2. Discomfort Rating; 3. *Sometimes Me-First.*

Three months and nineteen days later
Tuesday, July 26

As I was leaving my office, a dirty, unkempt teenager arose from the bottom step and started toward me. I felt my muscles tense and took a tighter grip on my purse and briefcase. When I was just one step above the boy, he spoke softly.

"Remember me? I'm Sammy Gordon."

He was so thin and sickly-looking I hardly recognized him.

"I guess you don't have any time ... and I don't have any money and ..." He turned to leave.

I put my arm around his shoulder and guided him back into the building. "I'm happier than you'll ever know just to see you're still—around!"

His embarrassed almost-smile told me we had connected.

Samuel Gordon Chart
Tuesday, July, 26, 5:45 P.M.

Freebie Session
Second Visit
SAMUEL (SAMMY) GORDON, 15 years old

"Sammy, I'm really, truly glad you're home."

"I haven't gone ... home. I ... I don't know if Mom would let me in."

"I think she would."

"But you don't know where I've been and what I've been doing for the past ... who knows how long."

"I'm positive your mom knows to the day and the hour."

Sammy took such a deep breath it was like he was trying to inhale the universe. "Do you think sometimes people can get a second chance?"

"Do I think birds can fly?"

"But I've done things I'm really ashamed of ... things I'd never want Mom to know about, and especially never, ever, ever my two little sisters."

25

"So? What's wrong with wiping the slate clean and starting over?"

"With me it would be more like starting UP, and . . . I mean from the *very, very, bottom!*"

"Everyone has to start someplace."

"But I've done everything . . . everything!"

"Not EVERYTHING, dear Sammy. You didn't 'blow out your candle.' I'm so happy for you and so proud of you, for that."

"Really?"

"Yes, really!"

"Do you think my mom could forgive me, too . . . and . . ." A stricken, heartbroken look crept over his tense face.

"And who?"

"God?" (He more mouthed the word than said it.)

"Have you ever heard the story of the prodigal son from the Bible?"

"Yeah, I learned it when I was little and went to Sunday school."

"Would you like to repeat the story as you recall it?"

"Well, this rich man had two sons and one took his inheritance money early, and went to another country and spent it partying and stuff. And when the money was gone, he couldn't get a job, so he tended pigs, and there was a famine, and he got so hungry, he ate the pig food. Finally, he got so down on his luck that he went home to his father and said he wasn't worthy to be his son anymore, but could he please be his servant . . ."

"And did his father allow him to be his servant?"

"No, he put fancy clothes and robes and stuff on him, and they killed the fatted calf, and they had a big feast . . ."

"And . . ."

"I don't remember what else."

"I'll tell you what else. The father happily said, 'My son . . . was lost, and is found,' and he took him back into his home and heart."

"I wish it could be that easy for me."

"Well, were you lost?"

"Yeah, I guess. In a way . . . from both my family and myself . . ."

"Do you think your mom loves you?"

"I know she did before I got so screwed up."

"If you had gotten *physically* disconnected some way, would she have ceased loving you?"

"NO!"

"I'll bet she'll welcome you back with joy and tears, and even pull out the fancy clothes and the fatted lasagna."

We laughed gently, and it was like lovely, bright springtime returning after a long, cold, dangerously dark, hard winter.

"What would I ever say to Mom? I can't just walk in like I dropped out yesterday and that nothing in between happened. I'm a different, second-rate, defective person now."

"Wrong! You're still the same fantastic person you always were. You just got your priorities mixed up for a little while."

"Will I ever, ever, ever be able to forget where I've been and what I've done?

"You won't forget everything in its entirety, but as you replace the *negatives* in your life, no matter what they were, with *brilliant-wattage positives,* the monsters of your past will slowly become distant grey shadows."

27

"I can't believe that's possible, not with what I've done."

"It is! Honestly it is! I've *seen* it happen more times than I can count! If any person really *wants to* replace badness with goodness, helplessness with helpfulness, failure with success, unhappiness with happiness, he or she can! People just need to be taught *how,* and then *do* the work required. The first and right-now question is, can you *forgive* yourself?"

"I'm not sure."

"Were you taught in Sunday school that God could forgive you?"

"Yes."

"I think much more often than not, God forgives people *but people refuse to forgive themselves!* Does that make sense?"

"Maybe."

"Will you ponder a little on that till the next time I see you?"

"Yes . . . but . . ."

"But what?"

"I'm still a little . . . no, a *lot* . . . scared and lost. I feel like I'm filled up to my eyebrows with . . ." (He didn't seem to be able to find the words to describe his load.)

"Garbage?"

"Yes, rotten, stinking, dead horse, maggot-infested . . ."

"I get the picture."

"There's absolutely no room left for anything good."

"Then why don't you dump the garbage?"

"I'd like to. It's like rotting me from the inside out."

"Well put, smart person! I think you know more

about how your 'YOU' works than you ever imagined!"

"Can't you just hypnotize me and wipe out everything in my memory for the past year or so, sort of like amnesia or something?"

"Sorry, but we've got to take it a little slower than that."

"How long?"

"Not very long, now that *you've decided* to recharge, rechannel, and upgrade your life. Actually, *no one else can do that for you* no matter how hard they try! However, any good, friend, teacher, parent, sibling, counselor, priest, etc., can help you make a positive alteration in both your present and your future if you *choose* to allow them to do so."

"I'm allowing, I'm allowing. Let's get on with my, from-repulsive-maggot-to-beautiful-butterfly-type metamorphosis—I hope."

"Sounds good to me."

"But I feel so unglued. How can I ever find the broken, lost pieces of myself and put them back together?"

"Do you think maybe we should go back and find out *why you made the decisions to do what you've done?*"

"No. No way! I want to forget all that crapola. I've got to get *on* with my life like you said I could." (Sammy began to look frightened, dejected, and beaten.) I want to start over new. I want to go *on and up, not back and down!* Maybe you can't or don't want to help me. Maybe nobody wants to or can!"

"You're wrong, dear, dear Sammy. I can and want to help you, but there's no way I can do it if you close me out. It's okay for you to disagree with what I propose, and I may not always be right in my assessment of a situation at first glance, but we've got to start somewhere. And I have a lot of training and experience in putting people back together who have felt fragmented.''

''I know I'm just a wuss being paranoid, afraid of letting someone else get inside my head.''

My hand reached out and patted his knee. ''You're a good kid, Sammy.''

He smiled. ''You sound like my mom.''

''I take that as a great compliment.''

''It is.'' He gave me two high fives.

''Let's try again to find a beginning place. That's often the hardest thing to do in a therapy session.''

''Okay.''

''Are you sure? *Completely* sure you can trust me with the hurtful, destructive things that are inside your heart and head?''

He hugged himself tightly, took a deep, deep breath and relaxed. ''Ummmm . . . I guess I have to, don't I?''

''Some people I see can start from where they are at the moment in their rediscovery and recovery program. They don't have to go back and regurgitate the past. With you, it's different. You have the equivalent of some deep, inner, abscessed wounds that need to be cleaned out before they can begin to heal. You've got to get them cured before you can proceed with the rest of your healthy, happy life.''

''Are you sure?''

''This session is going to be like taking out slivers. Remember when you were little, you probably had some big ones and some little ones. Some you fought having taken out, even though you knew they might get infected if they weren't removed.''

"I remember. Once I even had to go to the doctor to have him cut out a piece of glass in my foot."

"So? Where do you want to start? With the worst slivers or the barely-there ones?"

Sammy bowed his head and shriveled into himself. He seemed half as big as he had a few minutes before and about ten years younger. "I guess we'd better start with the big one. Everything bad and horrible started there."

"I'm sad that it's going to hurt, Sammy. But again, I want you to know I deeply care about you, and anything you share with me will be considered *absolutely* secret and sacred."

Sammy's eyes and nose started running in torrents. He didn't bother to wipe the stuff away as he began blurting out his story."

"I was a happy, sunshiny, self-confident, king-of-the-mountain type little kid. Even after we got the divorce, which hurt a whole lot, I felt I was special, and that I could lick the world at anything I cared about. I was on the tennis team, the soccer team, a partly A student, I played a little on a lot of musical instruments, I had two cool little sisters, and then . . ."

After about fifteen seconds I asked quietly, "And then?"

"And then that dirty, bastard-shithead . . ."

Almost instantly Sammy became another person, writhing and cursing loudly, incoherently, uncontrollably.

I put my arms around him in a firm, fiercely protective manner. "Shhh . . . Shhh, Sammy. Let go of the pain, the hate, the anger. Shhh . . . relax . . . relax . . . relax." I began gently, slowly, kneading nerve points in his shoulders, neck, and head. "Shhh, let the pressure, the rage, the tension, wilt and dissipate. Take some slooow deep breaths . . ."

After a few minutes the rigid tautness in his body softened into exhaustion. He looked up with embarrassment.

"I guess I'm not ready yet to face the hard-ass stuff. I had no idea it would be so tough to upchuck. One part of me wants to, but another part of me wants to bury all the crappy crap deep inside and never, never let it come to the surface till hell freezes over and beyond. The last part of me wants to snuff and get it over with. Does that make me paranoid and schizophrenic and other crazy types of stuff?"

"No, no, no, no. You're okay, Sammy. And you're certainly not alone in your feelings. Many, many people live all their uncomfortable lives trying *not* to face their pasts, or trying to pretend that the bad things that happened, didn't happen, or thinking about suicide."

"That's me."

"No! It's *not* you! *You* are willing to dump your past garbage. Together, we just made the mistake of trying to have you dump the biggest, baddest batch first, instead of starting with the smaller emotional bangs and bruises. You still want to go through with it?"

"Yeah, I do. I really do. I know I'll never feel clean and good until I get rid of all the rot-gut I've got packed away inside me."

"Would you like to pick a minor trauma to talk about and let the major one or ones sit for a while?"

"Like, just sit and rot and rust and disgust the guts of me till my whole me collapses into one thickness like a cardboard person or someone run over by a steamroller."

"Sweet, neat Sammy, it's not *that* bad!"

"Yes, it is. I'm a Humpty Dumpty you can never put back together again."

"Remember the little blue train that you read about when you were just a child? The one that said, 'I THINK I CAN! I THINK I CAN! I THINK I CAN!' AND HE COULD! *AND HE DID!*"

Sammy sighed deeply. "Well, okay. I was many, many miles from home when *it* happened, and all I wanted was just to put space between me and . . . the UGH. It seemed Mom was light-distances away on another planet, but I had to—I just had to get home to her and . . . it was like I was all the time swimming upstream—upstream with the salmon, upstream forever.

"By the time I got home, after three bus changes, and I don't know how many days, I was not only tired to death, I was hungry and dirty and stinky. I'd run out of money and energy and patience. I screamed at a guy in one station who sat next to me and dropped his head on my shoulder, and I cursed at the man at the ticket counter who said I was short twenty-three cents on my final ticket. I finally scrounged it up by going through every one of my pockets. I called him something I'd heard at school but had never before said myself. It was vile, but in some perverted way it made me feel good. Sick, huh?"

"Not sick, just acting out hurtfulness and sadness."

"I kept thinking that when I got home everything would be better. The nightmarish things would go away, and I'd go on with my nice life as it used to be." (Long pause.)

"What did happen when you got home?"

"It seemed like Mom was always ragging at me,

33

and the kids were nonstop screaming and quarreling and bugging me in every way possible. Even Dread Red Fred, who had become a wimpy dog, hated me and spent more time romping with my creepy sisters than staying in my room listening to the new Metallica tape I'd bought. I couldn't figure out what had changed everybody. I didn't know them anymore. They were like hateful, distrustful strangers."

"What happened when you went back to school?"

"My so-called friends had all become snots, snobs, self-centered, conceited, uncaring, unconcerned ignoramuses, jack asses all! I couldn't stand their guts. They seemed like protected little babies, only interested in their own sissy cotton-cushioned lives. They had no idea about what was going on out there in the real world. The thoughts made anger flame up inside me, hot and red as an out-of-control forest fire, wasting everything in its path, with me on the sidelines enjoying every minute of the disaster. My anger seemed like the only thing I could relate to and actually, in a way, enjoy. The rest of life was colorless, tasteless, odorless, drab and blah and not worth living, completely meaningless.

"After a few days I started wondering about the 'home boys' who sauntered up and down the halls. They seemed so secure and self-confident and protective of each other that in a way I envied them. They were not just single kids fighting their way through life alone; they were a solid, unified force. I wanted that kind of a support system. I needed it!" Sammy sat silent for a while.

"Before all the crap I had liked, *really, really* liked Harmony Harmon. We were close. Now she seemed like a holier-than-thou bratty bitch, always telling me to stop being so moody and so sarcastic and everything else. I didn't need her to swipe at me. I got enough of that at home.

"One day when we were out behind the school bleachers, she tried to snuggle up to me, and I was repulsed. It was scary because her touch had always been like electricity before. I pushed her away. Actually I . . . not just pushed her away . . . I shoved her . . . more like *hit* her . . . actually . . . *really* punched her hard three times! It was like someone else had done it. Someone else I didn't know, didn't want to know, couldn't stand. She felt it, too, because she ran away crying, 'You're not *you* anymore. I don't know who you are, except you're a pig, and I don't care if I never see you again. In fact, I don't want to ever see you again *ever!*' I knew she meant it, and I didn't blame her. She was right! Someone, or something, had taken over my mind, my body, my soul. I began to think I was possessed, taken over by devils, vampires, ugliness, evilness.

"On the way home I stopped at the bookstore and bought a vampire book and a 'possessed by demons' book. I was totally stunned by the number of books there were on the subjects. They disgusted me, but they fascinated me, too.

"A couple of weeks or months or something passed, and the supernatural became my natural. I combed all the bookstores for works on witchcraft and devil worship, convincing myself that I was just seeking information. Gangsta rap became my music of choice. One night I had a horrible experience that I can't even tell you about. It was real! More real than the experience I am having right now. I still get goose bumps when I think about it, and the hair stands up on the back of my neck. I knew I had to get out."

"Did you?"

"Yes, but then I was sooooo alone again, so empty. It was almost like being filled with blackness and evil was better than being filled with nothing at all. Life was so painful that it couldn't have been worse if I had been covered with boils in a solid mass from my head to the bottoms of my feet. No one who has not been there can possibly understand how awful it was."

"I'm sure you're right."

"It drains me to even think about it."

"That and the fact that you're hungry, and you need and want to get home. Do you think you're okay now? Can the rest of our inside cleansing, disinfecting, and deodorizing process wait until later?"

"Yeah. I really do think I feel a *little* better, that I kind of, in some small way, think maybe there might be a solution to my problems."

"Good. I'll drop you off at your house on my way home."

"Are you . . . sure my mom will . . ."

"I'm sure! And if there's trouble with money, don't worry. We'll work something out. In fact let's call this session a freebie. Call me tomorrow if you want."

Sammy smiled from the inside out for the first time.

SUMMARY OF SESSION

Sammy is home from a runaway experience. He is facing his past pain and fears heroically.

Working through general problems, past suicidal tendencies, experimentation with witchcraft, low self-esteem, etc.

Third visit
SAMUEL (SAMMY) GORDON, 15 years old

"Hi. Nice to see you back. I guess our relationship is secure as long as I don't let you go to the bathroom, right?"

"Wrong. My mom and I talked about my coming here long into the night. She's glad and so am I that *this* time I'm coming with the *right* attitude, that I need help and I *want* IT!"

"That's great! Because in the final analysis no one could *make* you change if you didn't want to. I gather things went well with your family."

Sammy looked embarrassed. "They welcomed me back with such love and warmth that it was like to them all the rudeness and crudeness and actual meanness that I had spread around and over them had been a bad dream or something."

"Soon it will seem that way to you, too."

"You mean we don't have to go on with all the shit ... I mean stuff that came after what I told you?"

"Well, no, we don't. That is, if you feel you want to live the rest of your life with the rotting roadkill of your past stashed away in the deepest, darkest corner of your mind."

He held his nose and shook his head no. "Okay. I guess I want to dump it once and for all if that's possible."

"It's not easy, but it is possible. And like I've told you before, as time passes the memories will become dimmer and less obsessing, until they'll be almost like the nightmares you probably had as a little boy after you'd eaten too much candy on Halloween or Christmas or something."

"Where were we?"

"On the evil demon planet of the black worlds."

"Oh yeah. During that stage I lost all feeling for everything. I was like an unfeeling, unthinking, unbelonging, unlovable, lonely—very, very lonely—and totally isolated zombie, one of the unreal, unimportant undead.

"Then one day Thing, a member of the Harpoon Gang, knocked me against my locker and tried to stuff me inside and lock me there. As he smashed my head against the shelf and my arm in the door, it hurt, hurt, hurt, and the pain *felt good!* It meant I was alive!

"With a type of anger and strength I didn't know I had, I fought back, bloodying his nose and leaving a big gash in his cheek from the pen I'd grabbed off the shelf. Thing began making cruel, deep, guttural sounds like an animal. That made me even madder. I didn't care if he killed me; I *wouldn't* let him beat me. The pain was actually invigorating. All the hate for myself, for the world, and for everybody and everything in it came like a mad, wild whirlwind of billions of years of unleashed energy that invaded my body. I was part of it, and it was part of me.

"Thing's gang surrounded us and all motion stopped outside our little orbit. Occasionally great gasps of terror or revulsion escaped from the uninvolved kids in the hall as blood ran and knees and fists smashed, with loud thuds, on flesh and bones.

"At last, when I was thoroughly intoxicated by the action and the attention, and I felt I had almost won the fracas, I let my arms drop to my sides and told Thing I wanted to join his gang. Immediately Slice pushed Thing back and took his place. 'Ninety-second Street Storm drain 10:00 P.M.,' he said. Excitement swelled up in me like an air pocket.

"I reported to the principal's office that I had fallen down the stairs, refused to go to the nurse's office, and started on my long walk home. People on the bus would not have been able to stand the sight of me. In fact the driver probably wouldn't have even let me on. Besides, I needed to walk and think. I'd heard about the brotherhood and belonging within the gangs, and I wanted *in!* I was beginning to hurt in every bone, muscle, and cell of my body, but I, who had always felt like a kind of immature wuss, now felt like the King of the Mountain, as I had as a six-year-old when we'd played that game!

"Later as I took the bus to Ninety-second, my feet and hands shook in spite of myself. Something inside me really didn't want to go, but something else stronger felt I had to. I'd heard how you had to 'jump into' a gang by fighting five guys at one time, and that none of them would let you fall down no matter how bad you were hurt. It sounded exciting, wild, and dangerous, crazy to the max. When I got off the bus, a cold night breeze had come up, and it made my pain feel interesting and somehow almost . . . creative . . . like a new part or extension of me. By the time I got to the dark storm drain surrounded by trees and bushes, my heart was jackhammering through my eardrums and for a moment I hoped my fight at school would be considered my initiation, but I knew it wouldn't be.

"The fight was even more brutal than I had supposed it would be. At times I'd almost pass out, or maybe would for a nanosecond or two, but the wrecking-ball fists of the guys kept battering away and the sounds in the background became more and more primeval, like the beginning of time in one of our literature books. It went on forever and ever and ever, and I felt I deserved every blow. I had to be a pretty rotten hunk of humanity to have had people treat me like they had.

"I actually don't remember a lot of the fight, only the hugging and the warm, belonging feeling I had after it was all over. It was almost worth the excruciating pain in my chest and my kidneys and my every other place. Some shit and beer and stuff appeared from nowhere, and pretty soon everything faded into one warm, stoned blur. I belonged! I was something! Somebody! Accepted and from then on protected, maybe among the lowest on the food chain, but still on it.

"I don't know how I got home except I vaguely recall guys laughingly dragging me into the backseat of a car and dumping me out at my place. Somehow I stumbled to my room and collapsed on the floor. My last thoughts were that I now belonged to the primitive brotherhood of man. I was a bro.

"When Mom came in to wake me up the next morning, she freaked out. She started yelling at the girls to call 911 and get an ambulance and stuff. I told her I'd kill myself if she did, that I had only been mugged. I said I didn't remember where or when. She checked my eyes and stuff, and crying and blubbering like she wasn't a nurse and used to stuff a lot worse than mine, she sponged off the dried blood and put ice packs on my eyes, which were so swollen I could barely see out of either one of them. By that time, both Dorie and Dana were standing over me and groaning and moaning like I was dead or worse.''

"Did your mom finally get you to the hospital?''

"No, I wouldn't allow it. I let her help me get off my clothes, everything but my shorts. I know she's a nurse and everything and has probably seen more male privates than most anybody, but I felt my privates were especially private, especially from my mom. For some stupid reason that seemed really important to me at the time, like that would be in some way infringing on the secret parts of my new-found brotherhood. I know that sounds dumb. But dumb at the time seemed, to me, smart. Does that make sense?''

"It makes complete sense, but we'll talk about that later.''

"Well, Mom finally got me into the shower with me clinging to my shorts like they were my lifeline, and she got almost as wet as I did as she gently sponged away the gore.

"She was trying to hold back her worries, but I stood firm. No way was I going to the hospital like a wimp after all I'd gone through to get into the gang. She helped me dry off and brought me some clean shorts and left for a minute while I put them on. I had to sit on the toilet, and it was quite a struggle to get into them because Mom was probably right when she said I had two or three fractured ribs and maybe a bruised spleen or kidney and who knew what else. Through the door her voice sounded wet as she pleaded for me to let her call an ambulance because she was much more concerned about internal wounds than external ones, but I wouldn't change my mind. At the time and place I felt I couldn't.

"Mom wrapped my rib cage with heavy tape, which about killed me off, and again checked my eyes to see if one pupil was more dilated than the other, and nine hundred million other things. Then she gave me a pain pill and warned me to very carefully watch my bowel movements, because if they ever looked black and tarry, that would be a sign of internal bleeding. I felt nauseated. No way was I going to check my you-know-what for you-know-what, internal bleeding or not. As I started to drift off into dim, delicious, delirious drug dreams, I heard Mom on the phone telling someone at the hospital that she'd have to take a few days off because her son had been in an accident. An accident? Me? Two worthiness experiences in one day. At least that's how I saw it at the time.

"For three days Mom *made* me stay home to recuperate. I was so mad and hurt that I thought I would explode. There was no way my namby-pamby mom and little sister could possibly conceive what I was going through. Nothing I did or said seemed sane to them. Grandma Gordon came to stay over the weekend, and she bugged me even worse. She talked and lectured and preached incessantly about changing my attitude, giving optimism and courtesy and prayer a chance, etcetera, etcetera, etcetera.

"She made me so nervous that I literally had to fight myself to keep from smashing her. For a moment that made me feel lonely because I wondered what had become of the sweet, innocent, loving, little boy who had once almost worshiped her. How could she and Mom and Dorie and Dana all have changed so much, become such plastic, gutless wonders, so unaware of what was really going on out there in the black, bloody, cannibalistic world that was just outside their door waiting to get them too?"

"At that time did *your* thinking seem right and sound and theirs seem completely off center and ridiculous?"

"Totally."

"That just proves again that people can be absolutely and completely wrong and still be sincere, doesn't it?"

"That was me exactly. I had allowed, probably even encouraged, hate and hostility to grow inside me like some mutated evil zucchini until it had not only taken over my mind and my heart, but my body and my soul and was now branching out to try to take over everyone that came close to me. I got so paranoid about that happening that I wouldn't let any one of my family get too close to me.

"On the fourth day I was still looking pretty scary and feeling pretty awful, but I put on my dark glasses and forced myself to go back to school. I couldn't let Slice and Thing and the others in the gang think I was a white, wisp wasp. Besides, my family was driving me crazy, pushing me closer and closer to doing something really demented. I knew Mom had called Grandma to come and just baby-sit me, and I couldn't handle that. I simply could not!

"It was great getting back to school. The gang accepted me as though I had always been a member. We joked and pushed and threatened each other in the halls, when no one was watching. Sometimes even when people were watching. *They* knew we knew who the watchers were, and they'd get theirs if they dared to tell. I related to my bros' feelings as hostile, unacceptable misfits, kids who had been cast,

43

through no fault of their own, into outer darkness, where they were simply trying desperately to find their own turf, to be respected, to belong. I don't think adults have any idea how important it is to a kid to feel they *belong* to something. Sometimes *anything!* . . . It's like . . . a . . . *when you're dying from thirst, you'll drink from a mud hole.*

"Almost immediately the gang became my security, my family, my life. We were one. One for all and all for one just like in the old Three Musketeers book I had read as a naive kid. But with us it really worked. They weren't just words. They were actions! If any of the other kids dared give us lip or even a demeaning look, they were well aware of the price they would pay. The whole school was in our hands, and they paid us respect with a capital R, like we demanded. We were lucky we were the only gang in the school. Other schools had more, and they were constantly warring with each other. With us it was just keeping everyone else paying homage.

"One weekend Slice suggested that on Monday every student at school genuflect to us. We got the message out to a few on-the-top-of-the-heap kids, and by the next hall time all the kids that passed us bowed their heads and bent their knees noticeably— even Chicken Little, the big bruiser football star, who had had it whispered to him that his legs wouldn't be usable for the big game on Friday if he didn't follow the policy. His head barely bowed, and his knees barely bent, but he still showed that he recognized our power. It was a rush. His dad was the mayor, and still even he knew where his nuts were stored. Wow! What action! What adrenaline! What power! What respect!" Sammy's hand flew to his forehead. "I can't believe this, but for a moment I was reliving the experience."

"How did that make you feel?"

"Like I'm two people, the then person and the now person." He looked scared. "Is it possible that I have multipersonalities?"

"No, but it should show you how powerfully *concepts* can control actions and thinking. It's like kids who are working their way through drug therapy programs having flashback highs just from allowing past *abnormal* destructive thought to control their *normal* presents."

"Will this go on forever? Anytime I'm feeling down a little about something, or I'm hurt or beaten at something, like tennis or soccer, or Mom rags at me or the kids bug me, am I going to revert back to my old gang mentality?"

"Not if you dump it completely after you've gotten it all out of your head and system, and you don't forever, or *ever,* go back to that toxic place to wallow."

"How am I going to do that?"

"We'll work on it after every last drop of rage, indulgence, negativity, pessimism, and venomous self-justification are purged out of your system."

He snickered. "Purged? You mean something like a mental enema?"

"I wouldn't have put it quite that way, but it is an all right simile."

"Maybe if I think of dumping all my past roadkill as a mental enema, it will help me do it better and quicker and cleaner."

"Anything that works for you, use."

"It's a pretty picturesque and gruesome thought, though, isn't it?"

"Not one I think you'd soon forget."

"I can't wait to get the maggot-infested yuck and stink of it out of my being forever."

"So you want to go on?"

"I guess it's the only way. Well ... I was talking about the flashback action and power and respect feelings. I'm sure they're all bogus now. It's like there are two sides to life. The good and happy and healthy bright light side and the dark, dreary, depressed, drag-you-down-into-the-depths-of-hell side." Sammy sat silently for a long time, contemplating what he had said, then he started speaking in a strange, almost-frightening, little boy voice. "Do you suppose that could possibly be true, all that good and bad stuff they used to teach me about in Sunday school? All that stuff about being on God's side or Satan's side? Are there any studies or proof of that?"

"I'm not sure about tangible proof, but there are billions of people in the world who believe in both good and bad powers. The Supreme Good Power is called by many different names in many different languages: God, Allah, Buddha, Vishnu, etcetera, just as the evil power is given different names in different cultures. It is also interesting that most major religions of the world have some form of the 'Do unto others as you would have them do unto you' Golden Rule concept."

"People don't seem to be doing very well at living that concept, though, do they?"

"No, but maybe that's because so many of us haven't had the 'Let It Begin with Me' mind-set."

"I sure haven't."

"But can any of us change our mind-set if we want to?"

"Yeah, I guess so. But like you've said, only *I can change me* and my attitude and actions."

"You're really coming along, smart Sammy. I'm very proud of you and very happy for your positive, progressive thinking."

"I'm proud of ... and happy for myself! Do you think maybe it would help me to get my life back in order and under control if I started going back to my old church?"

"That is a serious and deep decision that you must make for yourself."

"I wonder if God would *want* me in His church if he knew what an unbelievable person I've been ... what unforgivable things I've done."

"What does the God you believe in say about forgiveness?"

"I think the Bible has lots of stuff in it about forgiveness."

"The Talmud, the Koran, and most other scriptures do also. We've talked about this before. Maybe it's time for you to do some deep reflective thinking about your relationship to God as well as to all humanity. You know there is an old, old, old song that goes, 'I want to be happy, but I can't be happy till I make you happy too' *that* is a lot truer than most people want to believe."

"I think I believe that's true. In fact I know it is. I guess that most of us are just so busy trying to make ourselves feel good that we don't actually give a damn about how anyone else thinks or feels. That's sad isn't it, and selfish?"

"Again you're right on the button, Super Sam. You know, some people take years to gain the understanding you have. In fact, many people never gain it."

"I'm just sorry I've blown so much of my life and have hurt so many people."

Tears started rolling down Sammy's face and onto the front of his T-shirt. He seemed completely unaware of them for a long time.

"Sam, did you know that your tears, at different times, contain different chemicals? When you're crying for joy, for instance, like you probably did when you first came home and your mom and little sisters met you with hugs and kisses, your tears were vastly different chemically than they are now, when you're crying from remorse, or when you're crying from pain or whatever. Isn't that amazing?"

"Yeah, it really is."

"Have you heard of chemical depression?"

"Yeah."

"Well, interesting studies are being conducted *to see if chemical changes in the body cause depression or if depression causes the chemical changes, or both.*"

"You mean people can actually *make* themselves depressed to the can't-stand-it stage where I was when I wanted to ... to ..."

"Blow out your candle?"

"I can't believe the *real me* was in that tortured, defeated place. A place so dark and every molecule of my mind and body being eaten away that ... that, thank God no one who hasn't been there could ever conceive it! NOW you've started me thinking about something else weird. Are you trying to tell me that I took what could have been a medium sized depression and trauma and made it into something overwhelming with my self pity and negative thinking?"

"Do *you* think that's possible?"

"I'd never thought of it before but it kind of feels

48

true somewhere inside my head. *That's* even more disgusting than anything!''

''What is?''

''That *my* hateful, both mental and physical, abuse of myself and others, even before I got into the gang, was at least partially responsible for my downhill slide into ... the only way I can describe it is ... hell. I wish I'd known then ...''

''It's okay. Relax. You're never never going back there, dear kind friend Sammy, you're just going forward for forever from here! Now. Want to know more about the intricacies of the brain?''

Sammy nodded contemplatively.

''There are numerous studies going on regarding what causes what or what feeds what in depression. Great strides are being made relative to how the chemical balance in our bodies changes with feelings of fear, anger, pain, love, joy, etcetera.''

''Wow! Tell me more.''

''All right. The respected neurophysiologist Ralph Gerald said, 'Behind every crooked thought there lies a crooked molecule.' When asked if there is a chemical for every sadness, he replied, 'Every sadness *is* chemical!' ''

''I'm not sure I get that.''

''Then let me tell you a true fish story. Dr. Ray Fuller, one of the three scientists who worked on the drug Prozac project, tells of an experiment with damselfish. A number of them were kept in a fish tank with a barrier of transparent glass between them and some predator fish. The damselfish naturally thought they would soon be eaten. After a time, the serotonin levels in their brains showed marked changes. That simple experiment illustrates how anxiety, repeated rejection, and other things we experience or think we experience cause neurochemical changes in the brain. A similar experiment with mice and rats on one side of a transparent barrier and cats on the other produced the same neurochemical results, as did one with dogs and cats. Do you understand a little more about how *you* control the chemical changes in your body and mind now?''

"It sounds awesome, stratospheric, science fiction.''

"Science fiction it's not! What happens to *you* when you allow yourself to get angry or afraid or frustrated almost to the point of being out of control?''

"Ummmm, my muscles and nerves and stuff tighten up until . . . until they feel almost brittle.''

"What happens to your stomach?''

"It knots up and my heart pounds.''

"And adrenaline pumps into your body until the chemicals in every organ and molecule of your body are out of balance. Right?''

"I guess. If that's what makes me have muscle cramps and headaches and stuff.''

"What about when someone hurts you or humiliates you or rejects you?''

"I guess *they* capture me in their sticky black net, *or I think they do,* sort of like the damselfish, or the mice, or the cats.''

"Are the neurochemical changes in your body as real with imagined experiences as with real ones?''

"Probably.''

"What are some of the situations which might change the chemical balance in your body?''

"Hostility, fear, anxiety, feeling unloved, unappreciated, unworthy, jealous, insecure.''

"Do you think that other things which may seem

less significant might cause chemical imbalance also, things like low self-esteem, negativism, pessimism, hateful thoughts and so on?''

''Yeah.''

''What about when a person beats up on himself, or tears himself down, perhaps thinking he is not as good as others, as smart, as nice, as beautiful, as charismatic, as adept in sports, music, art, originality, creativity, or whatever?''

''Man, most of us must have our poor chemical balance popping and flopping up and down all the time.''

''And you and I must never cease being grateful *that our* chemicals flop back into the normal range, for some people have a chemical imbalance that they cannot control.''

''What happens then?''

''Medications have to be prescribed, some temporarily, some permanently.''

''Wow! I never realized *I* had such power over the chemicals in my body.''

''*Only you!*

''I wonder if my mom knows how much she lets me affect her chemical balance or imbalance.''

''You could talk to her about it.''

''I think a lot of nice things about her, but I don't often say them. I'm going to start doing that.''

''Kudos to you, kid. And what are you going to do about yourself, about your newfound chemical balance knowledge?''

''I don't know.''

''You know! I know you know! *You* follow the old-as-dirt and healing-as-sunshine AS IF theory. *You* act and think AS IF your positive, optimistic, loving, forgiving, patient, tolerant, helpful, compassionate

51

acts and words produce healing, balancing chemicals in both yourself and others.''

Sammy became very serious. "I know they do."

"Then you're well on your way to all the good places you want to go and the good things you want to be."

"I wish everyone had as much confidence in me as you do."

"They will soon. Actually as soon as you have confidence in yourself *and to the degree that you have confidence in yourself!*''

"I know it's not going to be as easy as it sounds."

"Things rarely are."

"I guess that means we ought to get on with the slop."

"Maybe not. It's nice to end a session on a good note where possible. You've got a number of positive things to ponder until next time, right?"

"Yeah. Chemical balance, self-confidence, God, and not allowing myself to get turned on by negative past experiences, to name a few."

"Excellent! You get not only an A-plus, but also a good star on the forehead. You'd make a good therapist. Maybe next time we should trade places."

"That would be a bummer."

I tenderly patted his shoulder. "I'm not so sure about that. You've got a lot of really good common sense for a kid your age, but then, most kids have a lot more sense than adults give them credit for."

Sammy grinned playfully. "Just so you see the superior *wonders* and goodness in *me!*'"

"Yeah, Smart Stuff. Each time I see you from now on, I'll *wonder* when you're going to take over my practice."

He stood up and hugged me, then pulled back. "I guess it's not okay to hug your shrink . . . not cool."

"It's about the coolest thing you could ever do when you're sincere. Smart people can always tell the difference between one emotion and another. And did I tell you about the Listening Room? You can go in anytime you want and listen over and over to your tapes. You may pick up some concepts you missed or just reinforce the positive things we've talked about. You'll probably learn as much or more from what *you've* said as from what I've said."

Sammy's forehead crinkled. "Don't laugh . . . but I'm beginning to think *maybe* I can be the same old nice person I used to be."

"Do you see me laughing?"

SUMMARY OF SESSION

Sammy has amazing perception and a sincere desire to change.

Material Covered: Getting into a gang because he wanted to "belong;" questions about God, depression, chemical imbalance, frightening feelings about himself, listening to his taped sessions.

Samuel Gordon Chart
Wednesday, August 3, 4:00 P.M.

Fourth Visit
SAMUEL (SAMMY) GORDON, 15 years old

"Hi, how are you doing today, Sammy?"
"Much better, thanks to you."

53

"Little thanks to me, mostly thanks to you. As I've told you before . . ."

"I know. No one else can change *me,* only *me!*"

"Right on, Dude."

"Right on yourself, Dudette."

A series of high fives.

"Guess we better rev up the old garbage dump truck again, huh?"

"Think we're ever going to get the thing completely unloaded?"

"Yep. I do now. I didn't at first, though."

"That's okay. The past doesn't count, only the present and the future. No black points for your past negs, only shiny gold stars for your pos present. You were telling me about how you were doing the 'Mom thing' when you were with her and the 'gang thing' when you were with them, but if you want to talk about something else—anything—it's as all right as all right can be with me."

"It's a strange thing about my mom. I always knew she loved me even when she didn't like me, or couldn't stand me, or was hurt to her guts by my mouth and my actions and my 'tudes. I'm beginning to really see how important pos 'tudes are."

"You're right on there. Many studies have shown conclusively and empirically that a positive mind-set not only can reduce stress levels and blood pressure, but improve work performance *and even slow the effects of aging in the body.*

"Wow! Like awesome. Tell me more."

"Okay, sponge brain, the army is doing studies on meditation to help soldiers' performance. Mental health and physical health are becoming one in Western civilization as they always have been in ancient cultures. Meditation, hypnotherapy, massage, exercise, diet, etcetera, are all becoming part of the complete package of holistic medicine.''

"And?"

"It's an exciting time. Body functions are being assisted by proper positive mind functions in all kinds of healing processes.''

"You mean a person with a pos attitude heals faster than a person with a neg one?''

"Absolutely, even in work with cancer patients.''

"I used to wonder why people were sometimes in therapy for years. Now I wanna learn about all the out-there things that I didn't know about that can put me back together in a better, stronger way. I just might become a shrink addict like people I've read about.''

"Not with me you won't. I believe in brief therapy, which means introducing people to the tools they need to work with, then letting them listen to their own tapes and build their own cathedrals. You'd be surprised at the staggering number of people who come to psychotherapists or even medical doctors simply for a friend, someone to talk to who is knowledgeable and not condemning, and who will keep things confidential. *Most* people just need a good, honest, caring, empathetic friend to vent with when they're angry, cry with when they're sad, commiserate with when they're hurt, be built up by when they're feeling insecure, and most of all, laugh and play with them when they're happy.''

"You're really getting me pumped up! I can't wait to get all the bad stuff unloaded so we can start packing more good stuff into my brain and all my other hidden inside areas that have been completely clogged up with neg gook for such a long time. I've decided I want to learn everything there is good about everything there is good. I've thought a lot about that the last few nights, and as I've tried to get my gonzos together in your Listening Room."

"Good for you! Lawrence LeShan, who was been pioneering in the mind-body discipline for years, says 'Meditation is a tool for your mind and personality, like the Nautilus machine is a tool for your body. Different meditations do different things, just as different machines do.''

"Man, that hits a harmonious chord in my dissonance-filled brain. Did you know I used to be really into music? I mean real music."

"I know and I'm proud of you!"

"My dad had a band when he was in high school. They played all over. In his senior year they even played on a cruise ship. That's what I always wanted to do as far back as I can remember. Actually I was fooling with the piano and drums and stuff before I even started school. Later Dad played with me and sometimes even let me sit in with the guys he used to play with in college."

Sammy's face fell, and I watched pain grip him like a huge vise. He still had a whole lot of imprisoning tension to release. For a long while he sat clenching his fists tightly and biting his bottom lip. His suffering was beyond tears. At last he asked in a dry, cracking voice, "Will I *ever* get over this . . . this . . . there are no words to describe it?"

"Yes, Sammy, you will. And at the rate you're progressing it shouldn't be too long."

"Where were we when I got sidetracked? That seems to be one of the biggest negs in my life now. I don't seem to be able to have a short-term and long-term goal focus, like I was taught I should have and did have when I was little!"

"We'll get back to that later. Okay?"

He tried to smile, but it came out all wrinkled and sad. "Okay, on with the show! But first throw me a life jacket of some kind. All the goodness has been squeezed out of my body. Please toss me the tiniest good thing before I go on with my self-torture."

"I'll do better than that; I'll toss you a humongously good thing—YOU. I haven't known you very long, but I see talents and possibilities and comprehension and kindness and compassion and gentleness and sensitivity in you that astounds me. *You will* get past this dark, dismal valley in your life. Don't give up. Never, never give up!"

"I won't. I just need you to help me exorcize a couple of hellish pieces out of my life."

"Do you feel now is the time to talk about that?"

"Uhhhh . . . no."

"Don't push. Soon you'll be able to see that part of your life realistically without the debilitating pain."

"You really think I can?"

"Yes, and I don't think it's going to be that hard once we get all the pieces surrounding the situation laid out side by side."

"Well . . . maybe I better go back to the gang thing and this time really stay on it."

"You don't have to if you don't want to."

"I want to! It's kind of like when you become a gang member you, of your own free will, give up your self-identity and become committed to being a part of the whole. Gang guys don't pledge their allegiance to their country, their religion, or their family—their only and supreme allegiance is to the gang—loyalty to it is first, foremost, and supreme.

"After I got a graffiti tattoo and started wearing

57

grungies and other ripped-off stuff, Mom stomped on my neck continually until I couldn't handle it anymore. She was always mad at me. My self-righteous, better-than-me sisters said every bad thing they could think of about my oversize clothes. Finally I couldn't stand it anymore and went on the streets with my bros.

"My biological family no longer seemed important to me, and I sure as hell didn't seem important to them. School and my part-time job, which had once seemed important to my overall future, didn't seem important, either. At that point only drugs and action upped me. The gang gave me the sense of belonging, security, importance, and pride that I so badly needed. Without question or hurtful comment, they gave me everything: food, clothes, drugs, alcohol, and even money. I felt they made me belong to a *real*, not dysfunctional, hypocritical family. They gave me pride and status. It was fun, action, mysterious adventure. I made a few deliveries for Slice, and that was all that was expected of me.

"I hardly noticed my transition from a middle-class, right side of the road, good student guy, whose English teacher had signed in his yearbook, 'SAMMY: One of my most gifted, likely to succeed students. Nothing but the top of the ladder for Sam the ham.' Now I was climbing the gang ladder. How much do you know about gangs?"

"Not much. In fact I've never worked with a kid before who was more than a weekend wannabe."

"Well, actually, the whole gang experience was much more scary now that I look back on it. I can't believe that *I* got so involved. But I was so depressed, so beaten. I felt like I was a 'throwaway kid' incarcerated in a deep, dark hole with no one caring, no one wanting to get me out. I was more lonely and desolate than you can ever imagine, suicidal to the degree that some days the only reason I didn't do it was because I didn't have the energy to take down Mom's gun, find the bullets, and pull the trigger.

"Actually I guess in a way I've gotta be thankful to the gang because they literally saved me from that. They aren't all bad like some people think. They took me in when I had no one else. They shared everything they had without question. They were my family, my bros and my sisters. I liked their motto, *por vida,* which means for life. I felt safe, having the assurance they would always be there to protect me. But I guess I better go back to the beginning and not ramble so much.

"Well, when Slice first said they'd jump me in I felt like a human being again for the first time in I don't know how long. I know that sounds crazy to you, but I think kids often rationalize that it's better to have a bad friend than not to have a friend at all. Do you think that's possible?"

"It's not wise, but I suspect it happens a lot more than most people realize."

"You wouldn't believe some of the kids on the streets in L.A. They aren't dumb-asses like I was, who ran away *from* everything positive *to* everything negative. Lots of them ran away from violence and abuse, filth and vulgarity. Little Spider reminded me of Dorie in many ways, yet her mom was a crackhead hooker and her real dad was a pusher who abused her in every way that it's possible to abuse a child. She lived all her life with drive-by shootings and rapes and muggings happening on every corner."

"I'm proud of you, Sammy, for being so sensitive

and having compassion for the kids you met who might have done better if they had known better."

"A lot of them had kind, understanding hearts beneath the hard, cold protective walls they had to build around themselves to survive. Some were even elementary school kids."

"I, with you, hope someday we'll find a way to get to the kids who are taught *that abnormal behavior is normal.* How can they possibly have any realistic concept of right and wrong?"

"I think I want to become a psychologist, so maybe I can help them."

"Then I hope you do, Sammy."

"It's so dark and dreary out there. *Always* so dark and dreary."

"You mention darkness a lot. When did it start taking over your life?"

"I dunno."

"Do you think the concept of darkness affects most kids?"

"Yeah, they talk about it a lot. Our music is filled with it and vampire books and other kinds of books like that are really popular."

"Have you ever heard of light therapy?"

"Ummm, no."

"I think it is one of the greatest tools therapists have. What do you think it means, and how do you think it's used?"

"Well . . . I guess darkness is the absence of light, so maybe light is the absence of darkness."

"Oh, Samuel Gordon, you're so bright. I want to screw off the top of your head and pat your brains!"

"You're embarrassing me."

"Really?"

"Yeah ... but it makes me feel good, too. Do it some more."

"Did you notice the lamp I have on a swivel in the corner of the Listening Room?"

"Ahhhh, yeah."

"You'd be absolutely amazed how, when you pull that strong light over the La-Z-Boy chair and turn it on, all the darkness in the room is pushed away, and try as hard as you can, even with your eyes closed, you can't bring the darkness back."

"This I've got to see."

"Studies have shown that people react to light like flowers react to sunshine. We need it. In areas where there is little sunshine there is a higher rate of depression. When the depressed people are taught to sit under a two-hundred-watt light for twenty or thirty minutes a day, it relieves much of their dark, locked-in feelings of despair. I advise all my clients, including you, to buy an inexpensive metal clip-on lamp to use in their bedroom or wherever. When the night bogies start stealing in, it helps drive them away in a hurry."

"It sounds almost too good to be true ... but I guess it makes sense."

"After we finish our session, why don't you try it for a few minutes?"

"I've been practically living in your Listening Room since I started coming here. I've used one of your little notebooks to write down the super stuff you've told me, and I'm trying to memorize and put all of it into my life. But you're really dumping on me ... good dumping though."

"That's the way I work. I offer ideas to you, and you choose to use them in your life or not."

"I'm using them! I'm using them! And I can't

wait to try the light. I want to know more about that."

"Another day. For now you're so bright and radiant that you're hurting my eyes."

Sammy got up and gave me a high five. "You're just trying to get rid of me. But I vill be back," he said with an Arnold Schwartzenegger accent. Then his accent changed to Frankenstein. "After I recharge my battery in your light la-*bor*-atory."

SUMMARY OF SESSION

Worked at putting Sammy's past behind him. Showed him methods for not being a *host* to darkness.

His personality and attitudinal set are blossoming. He is now an open-to-change-and-growth kid.

Material covered: "Pos 'Tudes" and their helping, healing power, also light therapy.

Samuel Gordon Chart
Wednesday, August 10, 4 P.M.

Fifth Visit
SAMUEL (SAMMY) GORDON, 15 years old

"Hi, Friend Sammy Gordon."

"Hi, Friend Dr. B."

"Do you know it makes me feel good to be around you?"

"You're just trying to rattle my cage."

"Uh-huh, I'm trying to release you from your cage."

"I think you're getting the dumb door open a little."

"I think *you* are getting the dumb door opened a *lot!*"

"I tried the light bit last week. I even showed it to my mom and Dorie and Dana."

"Yeah?"

"Yeah, they liked it as much as I do. In fact, Mom and I even hung a bright light permanently in a corner of the laundry room, and we put a beanbag chair under it. And you know what else?"

"No, what?"

"I'm ready to take my tapes home to relisten and relisten to them right there in my very own light therapy corner." He thought for a few seconds. "Maybe the one I'm going to make today I won't. I didn't think I'd ever tell anybody in the world about *that* descent into Hell that I *chose* to take. No one *made* me! I thought about it all night long ... a miserable night ... I'm soo ashamed. I hope you won't hate my guts when I tell you."

"I may hate what you did, dear Sammy, but I promise you I won't hate your guts or anything else about you. You're my true friend, remember? As well as my client."

"Well, like I told you, or maybe didn't tell you, one night when it was cold and wet on the street, Blunt (blunt is also a street term for a marijuana cigar), decided to hop in his old mobile and go to California. He'd lived in East Los Angeles originally and thought we'd be better off there. He'd ripped off a runner's small stash, so he thought we'd have enough stuff and money to get us there.

"Anyway, when we got about halfway to L.A. we had some car trouble. Before we got to the garage, he stopped a well-dressed man just coming out of a building. Blunt looked at the guy with the dead-eyed stare he had perfected. It was the gang leader's stare that most of us could never quite get. Blunt held out his hand, and the guy just reached in his pocket and took out his wallet. Blunt took out the stack of bills in it and handed the empty wallet back. It was almost a polite encounter between the two of them. Me! It had been a while since I'd had a mota (marijuana cigarette) and I was so scared I about messed my pants. Some hardened gang member, right?''

"You were just a scared, hurting, lost kid."

"I wanted out of there. Man, I wanted out of there so bad I could taste it, but after the garage guy fixed the water pump or whatever pump it was and we were driving down the road smoking some killer bud, (strong marijuana) it all seemed kind of funny, not wrong or anything . . . funny."

"Do you think you would have done the bad things you did up to that point without drugs?"

Sammy was quiet for at least a minute. "Noooo, no way. I not only wouldn't have, I couldn't have!"

"What does that mean?"

Sammy spoke as slowly as if he were weighing each word. "I think drugs kind of change the balance between right and wrong, yours and mine, good and bad, kind and unkind, darkness and light." He stopped for a long time. "I hope you never know how dark it is in there, and you know what?"

"No, what?"

"You don't even realize it's dark until you come back up into the light."

"That's beautiful, Sammy. It's almost poetic."

"Not to me it's not. To me it's ugly and dark and evil, and I'm glad as anything that it's in my past.

"Anyway . . . we pulled into the black, dark, scary-movie-like streets of East Los Angeles and even mj (marijuana) couldn't cover the danger and squalor and evil I could sense and smell."

Sammy's voice became soft and feeble, and his eyes appeared so dull that for a moment I thought maybe I should stop him. "Sammy ..." He didn't seem to hear me.

"I guess I stayed totally twisted (stoned) for the next century. I don't know how long. Dimly, darkly I can see drive-by shootings, graffiti paintings on warring soldiers' turf, a young boy hit on the head with an ax, a girl so cut-up in a fight even her mother wouldn't have recognized her. No one seemed to have any hope, not even me, maybe especially not me, at that time. We were all like a bunch of crabs in a bucket." Sammy seemed to come out of his trance a little. "I read once that gang members are like crabs in a bucket. Have you ever seen crabs in a bucket? If one tries to climb out, the others pull him back down again and again and again until he finally gives up.

"Suk was the eighteen-year-old gang leader Blunt knew. Three of his guys had fine buggies (nice cars) and plenty of money. The rest of us just ran errands to fulfill our needs. Everything seemed to center around a matter of respect. Respect for *what* I don't quite understand.

"To make a place for myself I pretended to be a Tijuana Mexican. My mom's mother was a Tijuana Mexican. She died when Mom was six. Then Mom was adopted by an childless older Anglo couple in San Diego. They were killed in an automobile accident when she was two weeks past her eighteenth birthday. She took what little money they'd left and went to nursing school.

"I don't think Mom was ever ashamed of being

Mexican, part-Mexican, I suspect, but she never seemed to feel comfortable talking about her past. Still she taught us to be bilingual from the beginning. In East Los (East Los Angeles) I hung with the Latinos, including Suk, and felt they might have been part of my primeval past.

"One evening as I stumbled past a very pregnant, very young girl, who had been bad cut (knifed) by either her husband or her lover or her pimp or her john, I almost threw up. Life had no meaning, no worth, there. People were all either too calloused or too afraid to do anything. They were like flies on the wall or cockroaches in the corners.

"One Sunday I graduated to crack. I know it was Sunday because I could hear the Catholic church bells ringing. Crack made me feel so good and euphoric that it frightened me. After a couple of days, I gave it up because the smallest pinpoint of something good in me said crack was the biggest liar of all. Whiningly I went back to spinning out on tabs and reds and bud.

"While on drugs, I could still semi-function, being a runner when necessary or, once, going with my *carnelitos* to rip off the wetbacks who were crossing the border. Most of them had with them everything of value in their lives, which wasn't much. They put up little resistance. I remember I felt so bitter and hostile, I almost wished they would, so I'd have a reason to act out my brutal feelings. Action was the only thing then that could bring me out of my lethargy. I hate to admit this, even to myself, to say nothing of you, but in some crazy, insane, demented way the evil little embryo of a satanic idea was beginning to form in my mind. I wanted to do a drive-by. I can't believe I said that! It was bad enough to have thought it.

"Promise me on the lives of your children that you'll never tell anyone what I've just said."

"Oh, Sammy, you know I don't have to promise on the lives of my children or anything else. I simply need to reassure you again that anything you say will forever be a solemn and sacred confidential disclosure."

"I can't believe that it could have been, but there were times when I wanted to feel the gun in my hand, feel the feeling that comes with ... snuffing someone. It seemed to give the others the greatest high of all ..."

Sammy began to cry pitifully. His body wrenched and shook. His eyes and nose streamed. A tiny childlike whimpering squeezed out from somewhere deep inside his tortured soul. After a while he whispered flatly, "Now you know why I wonder if even God can ever forgive me."

I grabbed his hands tightly. "As I told you once before, it will be a lot easier for God to forgive you than for you to forgive yourself. How are you coming along on that?"

"Not very well. If I could just rub out, wash out, scrub out, hypnotize out, meditate out, therapize out ... the evil gook. Have you ever had a client who had been *in* so unforgivably deep?"

"Maybe not in the *same kind* of gook, but gook, nonetheless. Gook that made them want to blow out their candles, too. It isn't a matter of which direction the pain comes from; it's a matter of when the pain gets so horrendous that it seems completely unbearable."

"Oh yeah, and at this time, PCP (an animal tranquilizer) was sometimes mixed with mj and *it* can really make people go crazy. Please tell me that is what made me feel . . . you know.''

''Is that what you think?''

''I don't know. I hope it was PCP, though.''

''Do you think you'd have felt that way and had those thoughts without it?''

''Oh, dear God in Heaven, I hope not.''

''You're basically quite a religious boy, aren't you, Sammy?''

''I don't think so. At least I've never thought of myself as being that way.''

''If you don't think so . . .''

''But then again, maybe I am. Maybe that's why I feel such guilt and pain. I hadn't always thought *wrong was right*, like some of my *carnelitos* (Mexican gang friends), so maybe . . . I don't know.''

''Do you want to talk about that for a minute?''

''What?''

''The difference in thinking and feeling between someone who knows wrong from right and someone who doesn't?''

''Maybe there isn't any difference. Yeah, there is. Some guys seemed to think that shooting on drive-bys was like shooting at bottles in a carnival.''

''How did you feel?''

''Actually, I only went on two . . . I think . . . and even though the adrenaline was racing through my body like strings of firecrackers and no one really got hurt, I . . .''

''You what?''

''Part of me really wanted to . . . be the one that *got* popped.''

''You mean, you didn't really want to do it to someone else? You wanted it to happen to you?''

"Yeah, I think that was it. Because my life held no meaning, how could anyone else's have any meaning or use or ... Oh, I was soooo screwed up, so doped up and screwed up I wasn't hardly even me."

"Who or what, at that time, controlled your life?"

"My good, God-given sense sure didn't."

"So?"

"I guess the dope did ... and the anger ... and the fear ... and the pain ..."

"And *who* gave permission to the dope and the anger and the fear and the pain to control your life?"

"I guess *I* did."

"Could anyone else have given them that permission?"

"I guess not."

"You guess not?"

"No! I know not! No one but me could have given permission to anyone or anything to control me, EXCEPT ME! I got so mad at Mom eons and eons ago when I thought *she* was trying to control me, even though she was trying to do it in a positive way. Then I stupidly and rebelliously *allowed* every sense and action and thinking process I had to be *controlled* by all the *negative* and *vile things* in the world! Actually, not only allowed it, but encouraged it!"

"Do you want to explore that?"

"Well, I was pretty put-together mentally till ... you know ... No, I guess you don't know ... *yet!* Anyway, in those olden days, so far back I can hardly remember them, I had friends and sports and music and my job. It was just a gofer thing in a medical clinic, but I liked it, and I had Mo ..."

"Mo?"

"Harmony." Sammy winced and bit his bottom

lip. "She was like the most wonderful thing that ever happened in my life. I ... I loved her. She carbonated every red blood corpuscle in my bloodstream." He winced again, so strongly it was almost like a small seizure. "We were tight as anything till ... I blew it ... like I blew everything else in my life."

"Why do you suppose you did that?"

His forehead wrinkled and his body tied itself into a hard knot. "I don't know. I had had *little* problems before ... you know ... but they had never clobbered me so completely or even hardly at all. Then suddenly and in one black whirlwind swoop it was like the whole world came crashing down upon me, covering everything, maiming everything, and a dark sulfur cloud squeezed me out of my existence into an imprisoned unrealness of fermenting hostility and pain."

"What do you mean, 'fermenting'?"

"Growing, taking over, souring. My life became foreign to me! I was part of the unwashed, the unwanted, the hated—a troublesome alien—and I seemed to be forever cloning myself into more unacceptable, unworthy, unhappy mes because the misery was too much for one young, stupid, helpless kid to bear. I know that seems crazy enough to have me locked in a rubber room in a loony bin ..."

"No, it doesn't, Sammy. It just means that the beautiful, warm, belonging, protective, brightly colored balloon you had lived in all your life, up to that point, had been suddenly popped, *deflated completely,* leaving you flat and empty. You had to, then, in some sense, *reinvent your life* and your place in it. It's too bad you weren't able to get help right then."

"Yeah, before things got so out of hand that we

may never be able to get my Humpty Dumpty self put back together again."

"Oh, we'll get Sammy Humpty Dumpty put back together again good as new, maybe even better. Never you fear."

"We've *got* to do something soon! I can't stand this pain and confusion and fragmentation much longer. I feel like I'm two people, the good person I want to be and the bad person *I am!* Actually I know this sounds completely out of orbit, but sometimes . . . in fact more and more often now . . . I feel like maybe I'm many different people." He started crying softly. "Lately, I've even started thinking of names for some of the evil entities within me."

"Do you think that might be feeding your problem?"

"Could be."

"Can it be dangerous to encourage any kind of negative thinking?"

"Yeah! We've gone over that!"

"When things get bad, have you ever tried silently singing a 'feel good' song over and over till it kind of kicks into your brain? Just to show yourself that *YOU* are in charge?"

"No."

"Could it hurt to try?"

"Guess not, but I can't think of one right now."

"Really?"

"Yeah . . . blank . . . except . . . this is dumb, but when I was little my favorite song was . . . it's silly . . . 'Jesus Wants Me for a Sunbeam to Shine for Him Each Day.' "

"What does that mean?"

"I dunno. I guess nothing."

"Ummmmm. If it doesn't mean anything, maybe it is silly."

Sammy became *very* serious. "No, it's not silly. Let's see. A sunbeam is part of sunshine, so probably it's warm and friendly and comforting . . ."

"And?"

"It drives out the darkness."

"And?"

"I used to like to sit in the meadow by myself sometimes when we went camping and just feel the warmth and brightness of the sun kind of hug me. I remember I could feel it almost like it was some kind of a soft, belonging, happy cuddling that I didn't ever want to stop."

"Close your eyes and relax. See if you can feel sunbeams caressing your face now."

After a minute or two, he whispered, "I can. I can. I really can. I wish I could just escape into that sunbeam kind of time-stands-still feeling forever."

"You can't do that. You wouldn't even want to. There are too many exciting, adventurous, creative, challenging things you still have to do with your life. But you *can*, on occasion, encourage yourself to take side trips back to that private awesome world that only you own."

"That's a cool thought."

"What does the Jesus part mean to you?"

"Aah . . . safety . . . belonging . . . love."

"Seems like a pretty good combination to me."

"This will probably sound disturbed, and I couldn't say it to anyone but you and my mom, but it makes me smile inside when I think of 'Jesus Wants Me for a Sunbeam' and old-time kid things. I'd like to be a good, clean, little kid again, now and forever."

72

"How does being a good, clean, *big* kid *now and forever* strike you as a cutting off thought for today?"

SUMMARY OF SESSION

Sammy talked about his problems in East Los Angeles. He wanted to get out but didn't know how. His gang's "turf" was its own country with its own laws and boundaries. He stayed drunk or stoned to exist. We talked about what he *might* have done, how negativity is literally a toxic poison to the human mind, and how he might choose a "feel good" song to replay in his mind when necessary.

Samuel Gordon Chart
Thursday, August 11, 7:45 A.M.

Sixth Visit
SAMUEL (SAMMY) GORDON, 15 years old
(Sammy called at 6:30 A.M. and asked if he could come in before school)

"You look as though you had a really bad night."

"I did that for sure! I think that the unbelievable, unforgivableness of my past is *just beginning* to really sink in! I had nightmares all night, each one getting more nightmarish."

"Come on, Sammy, you're supposed to be dumping out, not building up."

"Yeah, I know, but I can't make sense out of how someone who was raised in a loving, caring, privileged home like I was, who had friends and hobbies and everything that is supposed to make them normal, could go off and do the abnormal things I did. I wonder if there's something wrong with my brain, if I've got a tumor or weird chemicals or something. I can understand the kids who didn't know any better *not doing better,* but me . . . there was no excuse. I don't know how I ever got from here to there.''

''You got there one step at a time, precious person. One, sliding, downhill step at a time. You were suffering from depression, which is possibly the worst form of human suffering, and you began giving yourself constant negative conditioning until *you* squeezed out every bit of joy and light in your life! That can happen to *anyone* who has not been forewarned and forearmed about and against the *NEGATIVE POWER* OF NEGATIVE THINKING!''

''I wish I'd known *then* what I know now.''

''But you didn't, dear Samuel. That's why it is so imperative that we start emphasizing to people, especially young people, the *NEGATIVE POWER OF NEGATIVE THINKING.* Okay, so you, like millions of other people, during a *down* time in your life inflicted negative *thinking patterns* on yourself and *allowed* the negatives to grow until they took over—''

Sammy interrupted. ''And I *allowed* CR (CRANK chemicals) and sap (alcohol) to drag me ever deeper and deeper under, until I was not even hardly a human being anymore . . .''

''Oh, Sammy, I know you regret your past mistakes, and you should! But don't hoard them in your heart and mind so you can continuously wallow in them like a pig does in the mud.''

''I want to stop, but first I've got to get rid of more junk and more junk and more junk. It keeps expanding until I feel like I'm going to explode.''

"But we *are* eventually going to defuse your past! Don't allow yourself to think differently about that for a second."

"Okay. Back to East Los. I wanted out more than anything, *anything!* But I was afraid to leave and afraid to stay, and besides, I had no way to get out. So, I kept myself twisted and spun (drunk and drugged) to the point where I couldn't have thought if I'd tried.

"Then one night, I stumbled across a softly mewing, little newborn kitten in an alley. I can't remember where I found a carton of milk, but I got it somewhere and dipped my finger in and then let the soft, helpless little ball of fur lick it off. I hid the two of us behind some old crates, with him inside my jacket for I guess a couple of days. He just kept getting weaker, and I kept getting more in touch with reality.

"I couldn't believe where I was and how low I'd sunk. Sammy was the only important thing I had in my life. Oh, I'd named the kitten Sammy. In some strange way, he was like all the good things that had once been me. He kissed my face, and sometimes I'd put milk on my chin and cheeks so he'd lick it off, and I'd feel that I belonged to some good someone, something, somehow, somewhere.

"A few times I heard Cholo calling me. I suspected he had a run, but I didn't want to kick with them anymore, even though my stomach was growling from lack of food and my head was aching as well as all my other body parts.

"After a while Sammy died, and part of me died with him. I took off my shirt and wrapped him in it, then scrambled through the trash can till I found a little box his size. I buried him in the corner of the

75

bin and walked down to the church to pick two flowers to put over him. I was off my turf and was asking to get popped, but I didn't care. Most of me was dead already."

"That must have been inconceivably painful."

"No, actually by then I couldn't feel *anything,* but now I know *not feeling might be even worse than feeling!* Anyway, some forevers later Cholo found me wandering around looking for a way out and thought I needed action. I was too weary to resist. A few of us piled into his car and oozed around looking for trouble. Nothing much happened, and I'd just gotten out of his buggy when another car drove up and started shooting. They got me in the thigh and through my shoulder and waist."

"You were hit in a drive-by?"

"Yeah, and I went back and forth between being glad it was me that 'got it' and being in so much pain that I wished the shooters had done a better job. The guys wrapped me in plastic so I wouldn't bleed on Cholo's car and took me to General Hospital, where they unceremoniously dropped me by a side door. In a way I understood, because it wouldn't do any good for them to get themselves involved.

"After what seemed like another creation of time, with me moaning and crying for help and bleeding all over, someone came to the door and called for some other guys with a stretcher. They took me through endless doorways and then left me lying in a cold, drafty hall. People scurried back and forth, and it was like I was invisible. After what seemed like eternities I could hear myself sobbing like a baby and under my breath calling for my mom. Eventually two white ghouls stopped, pulled down the blanket someone had thrown over me and shook their heads.

76

One said, 'See this rag (bandanna showing a gang's colors)? These guys come in like flies. There's no end of them.' The other ghoul snickered as they pushed me into the operating room. I tried to get up to leave, but a big white-dressed refrigerator came out of nowhere and held me down while someone gave me a shot. As I drifted off I heard them talking about how bad I stunk.''

"You must have been grossed out completely by all that terrible negligence and inconsideration.''

"Yeah, and I thought, as I drifted past a blackness deeper than any blackness I'd ever known, that at last it was over. But it wasn't. Eventually I woke up in a blurred world of activity, people running around and pushing and pulling me from one table in a bright room to a gurney, then down a series of long winding halls, each having a different colored line or lots of colored lines running down its middle.

"After what seemed like miles, the aides stopped in a ward filled with multicolored corpses or at least different shades of black and brown and yellow corpses. It was more scary than any Stephen King movie or book ever could be. I waited for flames to start bursting up through the floor, especially after one of the corpses started making noises so gruesome they were otherworldly. I was rolled next to the noisy creature who was spewing up putrid yellow-and-green sulfur-smelling liquid that scorched my nose and my throat. I began shaking so hard I thought I would fall onto the floor until the two green-clad hospital staff members who had wheeled me in, pulled up the sides of my bed and sauntered away.

"The person next to me kept gagging and throwing up. His soft moaning and groaning outdid any sickening, spine-tingling sound effect movie studios could produce. After a while I wanted to get up and help him, but I was too weak. Besides, when I tried to move I could feel that I was tightly bandaged from my shoulder down to my ankle.

"At last the yellow skeleton next to me stopped puking and put the little metal pan he'd been holding on top of a table beside his bed."

" 'Are you all right?' " I whispered.

" 'Yes, thank you.' " His voice was little more than a moan.

" 'I ... I wish I could do something to help you,' " I said, from the very bottom of my heart. I wanted to go over and empty the throw-up pan and wipe off his plastic, tortured-looking Halloween face with a soft wet cloth.

"After a while he asked, 'Why are *you* here?'

"I was ashamed! 'I ... I got caught in a drive-by,' I said.

" 'Poor guy. Are you ... is it ... ?'

"I could feel his honest concern. 'No, they said one bullet grazed the bone in my thigh. Another hit me in the waist, missing my vitals, and one went through my upper arm, missing the bone completely.'

" 'I guess in a way you're lucky.'

"I shrugged, then realized how much that hurt. 'What's wrong with you?'

" 'I have a liver condition.'

" 'Is it serious?'

" 'Yeah, I'm just waiting to ...'

"He couldn't say the word die, but I knew that's what he meant.

"In the next few days, Ricardo became as good a friend as I ever hope to have. He told me how his mother was an illegal, but since he was born in Los Angeles, he had automatically become a U.S. citizen.

He'd had liver problems since he was a little kid and had always been sickly, so he hadn't been able to go to school much. His mom had brought him lots of books from the library every week, and a neighbor, Grandma Garcia, had taught him to read and write and think.

"I couldn't believe that he was only a year older than me because he looked like he was a very old, old, yellow, shriveled-up man. Outside he was scary, but inside he was the kindest, most appreciative, loving, thoughtful creature possible. He never said a mean or rude thing to, or about, the aides who treated us like we were scum, or his sickness, or anything. It made me feel like an ungrateful, self-centered jerk. I wondered what would have happened if we had been born in reversed places. He would have appreciated so much all the things that I had been given, and as for a dad, he didn't even have one. Mine at least gave my mom money to buy us everything that all the other kids had.

"I hated myself and tried to help him all I could, telling him about all the trips our family had taken to Yellowstone and Grand Canyon and Niagara Falls and all the things he'd only read about and dreamed about. He loved hearing about *everything,* and while it hurt to tell him because when I finished with each story I had to leave Mom and Dorie and Dana and come back to ... but at least I had him.

"Each day Ricardo got a little worse and every other day his mother came bringing him one single flower. I missed my own mom so much that I cried through most nights, but I couldn't let Ricardo hear me, nor his mom. She was as sweet as he was, and I was glad I could speak Spanish because she knew only a little English. She'd kiss me and hug me and thank me over and over for all I was doing for Ricardo. She had no clue how much good he was doing for me! I don't know how I'd have held together without him. The other four guys in the ward were tough, vile creatures who cursed to the aides' faces and spit at their backs. Sadly, I wondered if I would have been one of them without Ricardo's sweet companionship. I hoped not! I truly hoped not!

"After a couple of days the aides had me up walking with a walker like old people use. The four morons in the room teased me and waited for me to fall down, but Ricardo gently and lovingly encouraged me. I knew with his help I could make it, no matter what the other circumstances were.

"One morning I woke up feeling clammy-cold, and looking over at Ricardo's bed I saw that he had died. I don't know how I knew, but I did. Maybe it was the quiet, peaceful, un-pained look he had on his face that I'd never seen before. I didn't call for anyone because I wanted to tell him good-bye and how much I appreciated what he'd done for me and . . . how much I loved him . . . and wished that I'd see him again sometime.

"I spent a long time thinking about that and wondering if I'd meet him again in Heaven after I died . . . or if *I'd* get there at all . . . or if the Heaven thing was really true . . . or . . . I didn't have time to figure it out before the aides came and threw the sheet over his face and wheeled him out. A new kind of fear overwhelmed me then. I didn't know how I could exist in the General Hospital County Ward without Ricardo. It was a place where the welfare people and the street people and the like are taken. When I came in I wanted to scream out, 'I'm not one of you.' But I knew I was. Anyway, I somehow survived the next who knows how many days, till I was told I was ready to be released.

"One of the cold, unconcerned women, falling all over themselves in the office, asked me where I was going to go, and quickly I said 'the bus station.' She called someone to take me there and after forever an old greenish van lumbered up. On the way to the bus station I became frantic. I didn't have any money . . . and . . . I was scared. When we got close to a smaller branch of the freeway I asked the driver to let me off. I said my aunt lived only a block from there, and I'd decided to go stay with her. The driver didn't ask any questions. He just pulled over and let me off on the side of the busy road.

"It took a long time for a scrawny, scruffy-looking kid on crutches to hitch a ride, but finally a big, old, beat-up–looking eighteen-wheeler pulled over. The driver, as beat-up–looking as the truck, had to get out and help me up into the cab. He was so rough, it about did me in, but I didn't say anything because I needed outta there as much as I needed air at that point.

"The driver had a mind like a sewer and a mouth like an open manhole. He kept telling jokes and stories so sickening that I thought I'd throw up on my shoes. I used to think that was an expression, but believe me it's not. Later he started telling mother jokes, and I wanted to smash him across the head with my crutches, but I didn't dare. He was so big he could have broken me in pieces like a toothpick.

"A ways down the line he started talking about little kids, and I thought of Dorie and Dana and hoped the whole truck would blow up with both of us losers in it. He almost bragged about being a 'Chicken Hawk' (a pedophile; child molester). He

81

didn't deserve to live. Laughingly, he told me that I was too old for him, but I'd do in a pinch, only first he had to take time out at a rest stop so he could dump his lunch, and then we'd get into the bunk behind the seat and have fun. He giggled and showed me some hot Red Hair Sies (strong marijuana) he had and said we'd both take a hit before . . . His foul mouth watered and his red eyes glistened like the demon pictures on the covers of horror books.

"I softly said I didn't have to go, but the minute I saw him turn the corner to the men's room, I grabbed the Duce-Duce 22 (gun) I'd seen under the seat, stuffed it in my shirt, and dropped to the ground. I landed with such a loud thud that I was sure I had either shot myself or broken open my stitches, but I didn't care. I was out of the truck.

"Thank goodness there were high heavy weeds around the rest stop because by the time I hopped and crawled and belly-wriggled ten or twenty feet back into them, I could hardly breathe I was hurting so bad. I wanted to scream out in pain and for help, but I didn't dare. Ants crawled over me, and some big black bugs began gnawing at my uncovered arm. I didn't move, but occasionally, in spite of myself, the slightest moan forced itself out between my lips and I shuddered. I was trying with all my might to keep absolutely still and soundless. After a while I began to shake violently, and my teeth chattered so loudly that I knew the demon deviate would see the weeds rustling over me, but apparently he didn't because after a little while I heard the big old truck grate into gear and drive off without me.

"I felt a soft black cloud swirling around inside my head and knew I was about to pass out. I guessed maybe in a week or so someone coming into the rest stop, maybe the guys who clean it, would smell the stench of my rotting body and would come and find me. Maybe some wild animals would distribute my bones around the area, or a big dog from one of the motor homes would bring back one of my arms or legs or something to his master. That would be a pretty sickening surprise. It was horrible, more horrible than nightmare time, and I was so hot with the sun beating down on me that I thought for sure I'd gone . . . you know where.

"I decided that it was better for me to just do it to myself than to draw it out, so I pulled the gun from my shirt, released the safety, and put the barrel in my mouth. My fingers began to slowly tighten on the trigger and then . . . then . . ." Sammy choked up completely. After a few seconds he whispered, "I felt Mom put her gentle, loving hand over mine and slowly pull the gun away from my face. I did! Honestly, I really did! And she said, clear as anything, 'No, Sammy, not that.' She kissed me on the forehead and whispered, 'Relax, precious child. We'll be together again, soon.' I wondered if she meant in Heaven.

"I must have drifted off then, for I don't know how long. When I woke up the ground felt soft and damp beneath me, and it smelled good. Some bees were buzzing above me, and I was in no pain. I couldn't believe it and wondered if maybe I'd been there for weeks and nature had healed me up all by herself. But why would she do that? I wasn't worthy. I was a screwed-up dropout who wasn't fit for or worthy of anything. Why hadn't I just died like I'd wanted to for so long?

"I felt something warm touch my face as though it were gently wiping away my tears, and when I opened my eyes a sweet, bright little sunbeam was winding its way down through the leaves, caressing my face. Did it love me? Did one single little sunbeam in the whole world care about me, want to warm me and cheer me and lighten my life? I smiled and talked to her for a while as she playfully flitted back and forth in a radius of two or three inches but always coming back to *me*. She cared! That was enough! I had Ricardo and the sunbeam, and had it really been my mom? I fell asleep.

"When I woke up sunset had turned the world to orange. The leaves, the stalks, the sky, even my hand when I held it up was tinted with orange. I heard something rustling through the weeds and my heart almost stopped. What if it were a . . . a . . . Bears and lions and tigers and the driver and other unrealistic things flooded through my mind. Then I heard something whimpering and saw the head of a tiny orange-colored poodle. At first he was apprehensive, then he came over and gently licked my face. His tongue felt moist and sandpapery on my cheek and I heard myself giggling. This was a happy day. A sunbeam and a little orange dog loved me . . . and . . . maybe Mom . . .

"A soft whistle and an even softer voice flittered over us. 'Come here, Pumpkin.' Reluctantly, the little creature backed away. In a couple of minutes I could hear him whining and coming back in my direction. The soft voice was coming along with him into my broken world. 'Pumpkin, Pumpkin.' Asking the little dog where he was taking her, what he had found. A man's voice behind the woman's voice sounded not so pleased. 'It's probably just some old dead rabbit or squirrel or something,' he grumbled.

"The woman was more concerned and broke her

way through the weeds, talking gently to the dog and telling him to be careful. When she saw me she looked like she wanted to shriek, but she didn't. She knelt down beside me and cradled my head in her soft, grandma kind of hands. 'You poor, dear child,' she whispered, 'whatever happened to you?' Then she started calling, 'Karl! Karl, come see what Pumpkin has found this time.' ''

" 'Not another kitten for you to adopt, I hope,' he answered.

"By the time he got to me, tears were flooding inside me as well as outside. I'd tried to tell myself I wasn't scared and that I wanted to die and all those dumb things, but deep inside I knew I didn't, really. I just wanted someone to pull me out of my dark, mucky hole and clean me off and help me become the old me again. I clung to the woman's hand like she was my only lifeline, and I guess she was.

"After a little while, Grandma Maizy—she asked me to call her that, said everyone did—and her husband Karl helped me back to their big, beautiful motor home. It smelled of sweet things and had lots of pretty flowered stuff around. I felt safe.

"Grandma Maizy cleaned me up a little and fed me and pampered me like Grandma Gordon used to do when I was teeny-tiny. I loved it. Pumpkin and Shale, a cat bigger than Pumpkin, curled up beside me and soon, after I'd told my nice, new, pretend relatives about my *pretend accidental* drive-by shooting and my pretending to not have any family, I fell asleep. The last thing I remembered was the cat curled up by my neck, purring, and Pumpkin nestled by my chest, snoring, along with Grandpa Karl.

"I stayed with Grandma Maizy and Grandpa Karl for a couple of weeks or something. She washed and medicated and bandaged my wounds, and made me exercise a little more each day and eat right and all the things she had learned about health care over her many years.

"One day when we drove through a fairly big town, I decided I'd taken advantage enough of them so I borrowed fifty dollars and had them drop me off at the bus station so I could go home. I didn't really mean to go there but ... well ... I couldn't sponge on them anymore. And I did have their home address in some little funny-named town in California. I would have returned their money with interest, too, if I hadn't lost their address.

"In the bus station I looked over all the pamphlets and decided I'd go to Las Vegas, but when I went to buy the ticket, something almost stronger than me bought a ticket home (Sammy's hometown), even though I didn't want to go there. I couldn't! I thought there was no way that my mom and sweet innocent, clean little sisters would ever accept me after what I had become, the dregs of the earth or worse.

"When I got to town it was dark, so I dared to walk down my old street past my house. There were lights on inside, and I could hear music. Mom's car was in the driveway, and, as usual, Dorie hadn't closed the back door tightly, so the little bulbs were shining inside, running down the battery. I wanted to go over and close the door as I had a million times before, but I forced myself to go on. Mom's silhouette passed by the window as I reached the big tree on Mr. Laton's place. My heart was beating so hard and so fast that I had to lean against it to keep from falling down. Then I heard Dread Red Fred barking to get out. I could see by his jumping against the window that he knew I was there, so I started running away as fast as I could."

"Your pain and loneliness must have been intense."

"It was."

"So how did you get from there to here?"

"I slept in the park and then came and sat on your steps till you came out."

"All day?"

"All of probably the longest day in my life."

"You precious, hurting kid. Have you now finally dumped it all out?"

"I think so. Everything but *it*, that is."

"*That* we'll put in a separate department and take care of later if it's all right with you."

"Anything you say."

"Let's stop for a while and a little later put all the pieces together in the order of their importance. Okay?"

"What a relief it will be to finally be led out of my ... my yucky black past."

"Into your brilliant, glorious future."

"But I still feel like I've got fly-attracting crud all over me even though I've walked away from it. I feel dirty and unclean and unworthy and unacceptable inside and outside."

"Whoops, remember who is putting *those* thoughts into your brain?"

"Ummm, I guess *I am*, but they are just as real as though some unseen force had pushed them there and won't let them out."

"Then maybe it's time to face the enemy down and defeat it?"

"I'm ... I'm ... I hope I'm prepared for the battle."

"First let's relax and stretch and have some nuts and fruit and drinks."

"Sounds good to me. I need nourishment."

"Teenagers always need nourishment, physically, mentally, psychologically, and lovingly."

"Now *you* get the gold star on your forehead."

After a few minutes our session continued.

"We may be going over some things you've gone over before, Sammy Soul Searcher, but you've got to really believe in a principle and precept *to have you work for it and it work for you!* Does that make sense?"

"I think so."

"Then let's go back to the beginning. Where and how and why do you think you first began slipping into depression?"

"Well ... I used to sometimes get mad at a teacher, or ripped at my mom, or bugged out of my brain by my sisters, but I never hated their guts or wanted evil black clouds to close in on them and make them disappear or any of the other feelings that seemed to come over me after '*it*' happened. It really did seem that after I got black they all got black, too!"

"You felt and thought black and you thought *they* felt and acted black, too? You mean black in the sense of absence of light and love and good, shining happiness?"

"Yeah, exactly."

"Did you know then what you know now: *that people see others in direct ratio to how they see themselves,* in color, meaning, importance, feelings and everything else?"

"I've been thinking about that since you mentioned it before and I've accepted that it positively and absolutely is true."

"Gold star for you. Can you remember exactly when the unfamiliar discomfort took over?"

"Well toward myself and ... you know ... it came down in one black swoop like a bigger than person-size vampire bat. I told you that after that incident everything in life was like a slow-motion, old black-and-white late, late, late, late-night movie, didn't I?"

"What about other people? I mean besides you and—" I shrugged.

"*Everything* in life lost all color, even the trees and grass and flowers became black or dull grey. They were even more colorless than anything. Well, at first not my mom and the girls and my home and stuff, but they too gradually drifted down to nothing—sort of dark, evil shadows."

"Sammy, have you ever had ringworm?"

He looked startled. "Yes. Dorie brought it home from school once, and it spread like wildfire."

"Did everyone get it?"

"Yeah, some more, some less."

"Who got less?"

"I think me."

"How come?"

"I think by then we knew what we were looking for and caught it before ... Oh, I see what you're getting at. You think *I let* the black, disgusting, mind-eating ... begin ..." Sammy stopped and bowed his head until it almost touched his waist.

"Extending?"

"Expanding ..."

"Enlarging?"

"Defeating ..."

89

"Imprisoning?"

"Mind-controlling . . ."

"Ego-deflating?

"Confidence-shattering . . ."

"Distrust- and unhappiness-causing?

"Consuming . . ."

"Isn't it scary to think that the common, old, everyday variety of black *depression* can become completely consuming?"

Sammy's voice was little more than a gentle, pained whisper. "But only if I let it be. Is that what you're trying to get me to say?"

"Only if you thoroughly and completely believe it."

"I not only believe it! I lived it!"

I touched his hand softly. "I'm so happy that you're emerging out of your long trip through a tunnel of darkness. How would you measure the light in your life on a 1 to 10 scale today?"

"Where does . . . say . . . 112 grab you?"

"Right in my bright-light--, sunshine-, happiness-filled heart."

"Don't *you* ever feel depressed?"

"Of course! Everyone does! There are times when pain, sadness, emptiness, and/or depression are a part of each human existence. Can you think of some of those times?"

"For sure when parents divorce their kids."

"And?"

"Well . . . I'd feel . . . I don't know how I'd stand it if Mom died, or even Uncle Gordo, or Grandma Gordon, or . . . I guess anybody I love, even Dread Red Fred."

"What about when someone is treated cruelly or disrespectfully, especially over a period of time?"

"Yeah, or loses a job, or doesn't make a team, or

gets sacked. Man, there must be millions of things that could make us depressed to the max.''

"So should we learn how to handle trauma *before* it enters our lives?''

"Is that possible?''

"Yes, if we retain the knowledge that *any* trauma deserves time and space for grieving and healing.''

"You mean like a short time for a small wound and a longer time for a deeper one?''

"Does that make sense?''

"Yeah, and they should find a friend, a family member, a minister, a coworker, or even a crisis line to help them verbally ease their stress and pain so they *don't hold it in* until, like a pressure cooker, they explode!''

"Great simile, smart Sam.''

"Great because I lived it. Grandma Gordon's pressure cooker blowing its top, leaving all sorts of straggly, multicolored gook dangling from the ceiling. And the ringworm simile helps, too. We shouldn't *ever* let any problem multiply until it gets out of hand completely! Right?''

"Right.''

"Did I tell you that Mom once wrote in fancy script CHOOSING NEGATIVE PATHS CAN LEAD ONLY TO NEGATIVE DESTINATIONS and framed it and hung it in our front hallway, beside the mirror? That's kind of the same thing, isn't it?''

"Yes, it is. Does it make sense to you?''

"It does now that I'm getting my life unscrewed.''

"Good. Let's consider *what you might have done* at the time you gave up your free agency.''

Sammy thought for a while. "I honestly don't know.''

"It's very hard to think rationally when you're in shock, isn't it?''

"Terminally trauma-trashed."

"Not terminally, thank goodness. You're still here."

"Well ... I guess I could have ... I know what you want me to say ... *NOT* handed over to ... the monster ... *all* my thinking, rationalizing, judging, cognitive powers."

"Not what I want, what you want! Did you at the moment of trauma *GIVE* him your remote control ability?"

"Absolutely and completely, I allowed him to make me a hate-filled clone monster just like him, always looking for the negative, not caring about anyone else's feelings or wants or needs."

"Do I hear you saying that after that you began hating, not only him, but everyone, including your neighbor as yourself, instead of following the Biblical teaching of loving your neighbor as *yourself*?"

"I hate to admit it, but that's true."

"What if you had *put your emotions* on *hold* long enough for you to talk to someone and ease your pain. Suppose you had *taken time out* to recognize '*him*' doing his thing, as the evil, terrible, BAD THING it was, with you still continuing to *love and respect yourself* enough to go on with your doing your good, loving things?"

"Maybe if I'd known then what I know now I *could* have seen him as the thoroughly crazy, lunatic, every single which way demented abuser ..." He hesitated. "*Abuser ... loser .. abuser* he is, and not let *him* rub off on me; making *me* feel too dirty and disgusting to live on the planet!"

"And you could have thereby controlled some of the contagious, debilitating hate and disrespect for both yourself and others that began *taking over* your thinking. Right?"

"Probably . . . absolutely. If I had just retained command of my thinking and actions, instead of giving that power to the person who deserved it least . . . man . . . it was stupid of me to have tried to O.D. and become a complete hog-head just because *he was one.*"

"And . . ."

"I'd have *not* stopped using my brain just because he had stopped using his."

"Good! Have you ever thought about how much energy it takes to HATE? *Energy that should be spent on loving, caring, helping, healing. All the things that make others, as well as oneself, happy, belonging, nestled harmoniously into the environment.*"

"Hadn't thought about it . . . but it feels true. A teacher, or someone, once told us that *'if you aren't happy and at peace with the place or the people where you are, you aren't going to be happy and at peace with yourself or the people where you're going, no matter where it is.'* "

"That, as you say, 'feels true to me.' "

"I wonder if trying to have love and hate in your life at the same time isn't about as impossible as a bird trying to fly up and down at the same time."

"Which do you think is the stronger force?"

"I suspect love would be if we'd let it."

"I agree. I believe love and respect for self and others is the answer to the world's problems, as well as to our own."

"I wish like everything that I'd gotten out of that hellhole and gone back to Mom's when I first sensed that I was in a dangerous situation."

"Do you think next time you're in a traumatic predicament you can be in control of *yourself* instead of allowing them or it, whoever or whatever, to control you?"

"I hope I'll never have to face anything like that in my life again."

"Probably not exactly like that, but you will face other difficult situations, everyone does."

"Well . . . I may not handle all situations perfectly in the future, but I certainly will be more prepared to keep my control buttons to myself."

"Then you've learned one of the greatest lessons anyone can learn!"

"Just too bad I had to learn it in such a hard way."

"If you're sure you've learned how to respect and appreciate your absolute and sacred *self-control mechanism* which *no one else* should ever be allowed to master, except you, we will soon be ready to go on to dumping the last of the putrefying garbage of your past once and for all."

Sammy looked pained. "One more thing. I'm not sure how I'll face . . . school on Monday. Trying to go from the gang thing back to my old friends isn't going to be that easy."

"None of us were ever told that life would be easy, *only that it would be worth the effort!* What about telephoning a couple of your old buddies, explaining what has happened in your life—of course, without gory specifics—and asking them to forgive you and accept you back as a friend?"

"That sounds more scary than . . . most anything. Got any other bright suggestions?"

"No. Sooner or later you're going to have to, one way or another, face those you've hurt or embarrassed or whatever and make amends and rebuild bridges. I know you can do it! You're a bright kid, and you deserve better than what you have mainly dealt out to yourself."

"You can say that again."

"Okay. You're a bright kid and you deserve . . ."

"Enough, already. I'll try. No! I'll do it. I'll talk to the principal, and I'll get my mom or someone to take me to school and bring me back, and I'll . . ."

Sammy shuddered. He was wondering, as was I, if the gang would make him "jump out" as he had jumped in—with a merciless beating by five gang members. I doubted he could stand such punishment in his weakened state and suggested maybe he should have home schooling for a while.

He grinned from ear to ear. "No thanks! Say good-bye to the *new* Smiling Sunshine Sam who is going off to fight and win both his physical and mental wars by himself." He crossed his heart. "I hope!"

SUMMARY OF SESSION

Giving away personal self-control buttons.

Facing being "jumped out" of a gang.

Possibility of home schooling.

Calling an old friend, explaining his past, and asking for support.

Samuel Gordon Chart
Wednesday, August 24, 4:30 P.M.

Seventh Visit
SAMUEL (SAMMY) GORDON, 15 years old

"Yo, Sammy. You look great."

"You mean like you weren't expecting to see me all in one piece?"

"Hey, I wish you hadn't asked that question."

"I knew you were worried about the 'gang thing,'

and don't think I wasn't! I've heard some pretty scary stories about kids trying to be 'jumped out' of a gang. I wasn't too concerned about the other stuff. Actually everything went even smoother than I ever dreamed it could. Probably because like you suggested, I called my friend Marv, who I've known since we were in grade school, and told him just a little about what a mixed-up, screwup I'd been. I told him, too, how I wanted to repent and come back. I used the word 're-pent' because we used to go to Sunday school together sometimes when we were little.

"We blabbed for hours, talking about our nutty old English teacher who made us read gooey poems by Elizabeth Barrett Browning in front of the class, and the time we were playing team tennis and I came up behind him for a ball, and his backswing hit me in the head so hard that I googled out on the court. We laughed till we cried. It was wow! And I really did feel like maybe someday I would be able to live back in the olden, no hassle, no hang-up days."

"I knew you could do it."

"I don't think I could have done it without know-ing that you knew I could do it before *I* even knew I could do it."

"It looks like you've still got some work to do in the self-esteem, self-confidence area, *BUT* I'll be be-hind you; your coach, your mentor, your pep squad, your leader, your teacher, your booster, your admirer, your I-know-you-can-do-it, your positive thinker, your light turner-onner. All those things and more. Also I'll give you a couple of books that will help you to *help yourself* if you'll let them."

"Adults have a lot of self-help books, but I've never seen one especially for kids. Why don't you write a self-help book just for kids?"

"If I ever do, I'll dedicate it to *you,* promise! Now on with *your* life."

"Well, after I talked to Marv I felt so good I called Tommy Tompkins. He's always been like the major class clown. Me and him have been buds for years, too. For the first few minutes after I called, Tommy and I were both kind of uncomfortable, and his sister kept bugging him for the phone, but when we finally got to really talking from our guts, it was stratospheric. He understood more than I ever thought he could, and he said he wanted more than anything else to be my friend again and to help me get better in my head and my heart."

"It's wonderful to have friends like that, isn't it?"

"It's more wonderful than almost anything else except family."

"But one has to *be* a friend to have a friend, don't they?"

"I'd never thought about that before, but it's true, isn't it? You can't expect anyone to really like and respect you unless you first like and respect them."

"And unless you really *like and respect yourself!* Right?"

"Ummm, yeah . . . probably."

"Could that be the main reason why some people have many friends and some people have few or none?"

"Could be. Could be! I'll need to think on that some."

"We could spend a whole session on more security, belonging, comfort-level concepts like that, but hadn't we better get back to school things?"

"Well, I hadn't slept a full night since I got home I was so, in a part of me, worried about the gang thing. My stitches had all been removed, but I still had red shriveled-looking scars where the wounds were trying to heal. Actually I'd had some infection that Grandma Maizy had cleared up, but I still don't feel quite up to snuff, and I still have to baby my right leg some. I wondered if the scars would all break open if I got pounded pretty good, which I was almost sure I would. It was kind of a nightmarish time."

"You poor kid. I can't imagine a more nightmarish time. You must have been really scared and uncertain."

"Yeah, I was, till Marv told me they had a new principal at our school and that he had insisted all the troublemakers be sent to the alternative school that our town had been talking about since as long ago as I can remember. That really took the bricks out of my belly."

"It takes a few out of mine, too."

"I wish I could talk to everyone like I talk to you. I open my mouth and just let my tongue wag and my brains fall out."

"Most of that is because you trust me. You know I wouldn't betray your confidence. Wouldn't life be wonderful if we could feel safe and secure with everyone? If we could say whatever we thought without having someone be critical or infer that they knew better, or reasoned more deeply, or were better read, or that we had intentionally hurt their feelings, etc? I'm grateful and flattered that you can 'let your brains fall out' with me. I hope you'll never forget that, as I've told you before, I'm always as near as your phone."

"You don't know how much security that's given me after all my super insecure hard times."

"I'm glad."

"Let me tell you about Dr. Davidson, the new principal. He's spent a lot of time with me. He's

African American and he's about the straightest arrow I've ever met. He's a kind of hard as the Rock of Gibraltar type guy, but gentle as a kitten at the same time. Does that make sense?"

"The kindest kind of sense."

"And you know what's funny?"

"No, what?"

"He used to be a gang member, too, but he was different than me. He grew up on the tough side of Chicago, and he had to scrounge to exist. His mom was a maid who had to take the bus across town every day and work from early morning till late at night. His dad? He had no idea who he was, and his grandma mostly raised him. Dr. D. said he'd never told anyone else at school the details of his background, but he seems to feel about me like I feel about him. In fact, a couple of times I've found myself imagining that he was taking me under his wing ... and even ... that he was my dad. Is that totally insane or what? I wasn't going to tell you that because I hoped you thought that I was getting my gonzos together and doing pretty well."

"I do! And I did! It's perfectly all right and normal for you to have a pretend father when you don't have a real father figure in your life. Actually, in one study, groups of young men who had lived in boys' homes, during part or all of their growing up years, were interviewed as adults. Each of them said that at one time or another during their stay they had envisioned Matthew Marcus, the compassionate supervisor of the program, as their father."

"Whew. It's a relief to know that at least in one area I'm normal."

"You're more normal than you like to believe.

Actually what is normal? It's *not* a small, restrictive cage!"

"Is it normal to think you're not normal?"

"Very normal! Especially if you're young! And don't worry about it. If you're trying to be nourishing to yourself as well as to others, and you keep a *happy, pos 'tude, you can always* rest assured that you'll be *more* normal than most normal folks."

"Okay, back to Dr. Davidson. In some ways he's not like me at all. He had nothing, and he clawed his way up to what he calls his 'Plateau of Contentment.' Me, on the other hand, I had everything, and I willingly chose to take the dark, downhill route to complete discontent and self-destruction.

"I honestly almost can't believe I did those things now. But the black hate in my heart just kept exploding in greater and greater detonations until I was no longer *ME! IT* was *ME!* Why hadn't I been taught somewhere along the line that hate could grow like that?"

"Would you have believed your mom or anybody else if they had told you?"

"Probably not."

"How about you and I go on a crusade to teach everyone how quickly negative thoughts and actions *can* contaminate, actually toxically poison?"

"I sure could have saved myself a lot of pain if I'd known way back then how insidiously"—a half smile crossed his face—"that was a spelling word I missed twice and thought I'd never use but it fits exactly here, anyway *I can't believe how quickly my self-esteem was replaced by self-hatred, which then took over every part of my body—physically, mentally, emotionally and spiritually.*" He shuddered, "Do you think it could happen to me again?"

"What do you think?"

"It's scary, and I don't want to believe it, but I think it could . . . IF I'D LET IT! WHICH I WON'T! Never, never, in my life again will I let negativity, or pessimism or depression or any of the other black destroying monsters of my past be in control of me! I'll recognize them and stamp them out like black widow spiders while they're still eggs, and while I'm still in control."

"Dear, dear, Sammy, do you realize how deep and accurate that statement is?"

"You mean that I must learn to control depression and hostility or they will control me?"

"Absolutely true. I stand amazed by the simple, down-to-earth, awesome insight that teenagers often have."

"That's refreshing. Most adults think we're just a crop of no-brainers."

"Only some adults think that. The silent majority of us respect the greater part of your generation and what you have to offer our future as well as yours."

"Thanks. I was telling you about Dr. Davidson, the coolest of all cool principals. He was brought up in a cement and asphalt jungle, in the crime-infested part of Chicago. Anyway, his grandma and mom would hardly let him out of their sight till he started school. By then he'd had a little four-year-old cousin killed in the cross fire from a gang shoot-out, and the little kid had just been playing on the steps in front of her house. He had two uncles in jail and others in gangs and drug dealing.

"And some of his aunts and their girl kids. He got tears in his eyes the only time he ever mentioned them to me. Very young girls to women who 'had babies and babies and more babies.' Poor Dr. Davidson, he had been to five relatives' funerals by the

101

time he was in junior high school, and most of the deaths had been gang- or drug-related in one way or another.

"Dr. D.—I call him that when the two of us are alone, not when we're around anyone else; I guess it makes me feel closer to him and safer, in some crazy way. Anyway, he said one day when he was ill, he was sitting on their front stoop and he knew his grandma was watching him out the window. He got so mad he just wanted to get up and run down to the corner where a bunch of guys were hanging, laughing and dancing to a boom box and shoving each other playfully and sometimes sharing a joint. He got up and started to do it. He was tired of his mom and grandma making him study every night when no one else had to and tired of always being with one of them, never having a life of his own. He had nothing. The street guys had everything—fun, friendship, freedom!

"But when Dr. D. thought *freedom*, it was like some literal force pulled him back, sat him down on the stoop, and pried open his brain. Positive thoughts poured in, pushing away the negative ones. Did he really want to wind up on the street like his dead relatives, or the pushers or the runners or the gang-bangers or the alcoholics or the crack addicts? All the fears that possessed him and his mom and his grandma, when there was a shooting on the street outside his home, pulled in on him. Often the three of them huddled together in his grandmother's little room, which was on the inside of the building where stray bullets couldn't come through.

"Dr. D. said his teachers had to spend so much time just keeping, or at least trying to keep, order that they were more like policemen than teachers.

Each one of his classes was mainly a daily exercise in crowd control. He and the few other kids who were interested in learning were in the minority, and the street culture was as noticeable inside the building as outside. Actually, in many ways, the few good students were in more danger inside the school than outside. They were teased, tormented, and sometimes even tortured. Dr. D. pulled up his shirt and showed me lots of 'jabber' scars he had received in the school halls and on the grounds, when the kids used to wear Afros."

"What is jabber?"

"I asked that, too. It's sort of like a metal fork, but of course stronger and with longer and sharper points. If a kid was caught with one he, or she, would claim it was a hair pick, but usually kids who were jabbed didn't dare leak it to anyone. That would have brought down more torment. Dr. D. said good students attracted all kinds of bullying. He even had kids threaten to shoot or cut (stab) him when he got 100 percent on tests. In fact, at one point it got so bad, he purposely missed many questions. In one class while he was in high school his teacher understood and told him that when it came time for his college admission, she would write a long letter on his behalf and have the other teachers and the principal sign it. He said the worst thing is that things are worse today than they were then."

"What a travesty of justice and honor and education. It makes me sad."

"What would you have done if you had been there?"

"I would have tried!"

"He said lots of them tried. One teacher, Mr. Pliede, in high school became his hero. He encouraged Dr. D. and gave him extra credit assignments that no one else ever saw. He drilled him and challenged him in other subjects and even bought him an exercise video so that he could exercise at home and wouldn't have to go out on the streets.''

"Wasn't Dr. Davidson fortunate to have had Mr. Pliede, and aren't you fortunate to have *him?*"

"Yeah, but sometimes it makes me feel even more guilty, me having everything and screwing up, and him having nothing and shooting straight.''

"Sammy, there is an old, old, old saying, 'Don't cry over spilled milk.' Think about that for a few seconds. Does it make sense?''

He laughed. "I guess it means what's over is over and you can't pick up milk.''

"So?''

He was quiet for a while. When he spoke his face was serious and tense. "I just wonder what would have happened to weak-kneed me if I'd been brought up in Dr. D.'s place.''

"Don't! Just bring out your trusty old pos 'tude ladder and start climbing up, up, up and out of your dark restrictive hole into the pos 'tude of your bright unrestricted peace and personal fulfillment.''

"That sounds good *for me* but it makes me even sadder for all the hurting kids who seem stuck in their dead-end situations. I wish like everything there was something I could do for *them!*''

"There are many things you can do for them, dear Sammy.''

Sammy grunted wearily.

"There are many things we all could, and should, be doing. For instance there are remedial reading, writing, and arithmetic classes in many libraries around the country, including school libraries.''

"Really?''

"Really! And they are ever so important because according to the latest statistics between ten and thirteen percent of Americans are functionally illiterate. That means they read at, or below, a third grade level, or not at all."

Sammy's eyes opened wide with shock, then he smiled. "Wow, imagine the excitement and adventure that would be brought into a person's life if they were taught how to make thoughts and concepts out of squiggly lines."

"Imagine!"

"Maybe Dr. Davidson could connect me with a kid who is behind and I could tutor him before or after school. Maybe I could even become a 'big brother' to a kid from a broken family."

"Isn't it exciting to know that *you* can make a difference?"

"And *I will* do something! I don't understand how in the past I could have been given so much and have given so little in return!"

"It doesn't make sense to *dwell* on negatives either. *So* what positive thing are we going to do first?"

"I dunno."

"Then I've been wasting my time, and your time and money."

"That's not so! Mmmm . . . I guess . . . no! I think . . . no! I *know* each of us has to first help ourselves up to a good mental health plateau so we can then help others and hopefully, in time, our pos 'tudes will spread out like waves on a pond and the world will be engulfed by them." Sammy shrugged and looked sad. "At least they'll be able to engulf a few people. Some people are so far gone I don't know about them."

"Want to talk about *them* for a minute?"

"You mean like I was one of *them* at one time?"

"I didn't say that, you did."

"Well . . . let's take Casey Millburn in my class. He's a smart-ass if there ever was one. I'm not sure anyone, anywhere, anytime could ever help him. He's a bully. He bosses everyone around. He thinks he's been elected dictator of the universe since the gangs left. He lords it over everyone and pretends he's always right, always best, always in charge, on top, the greatest of all great Moo Goo's."

"Is there a possibility that he might have a low self-esteem problem?"

"Cardboard Casey? Low self-esteem? Are you out of your mind?"

"*Clear your mind* for a moment and think about this: Is it possible that Casey's outrageous behavior might be because *he has zero self-esteem?*"

"No way! If anything he's got too much self-bloating self-esteem. What I think he needs is stiffer consequences when he gets out of hand. Mr. smart aleck, show-off, better-than-anyone-else tough guy needs a little humility knocked into him."

"But what if the arrogance, the bullying, the bragging *aren't* signs of self-esteem?"

"Well . . ."

"What if Casey's *feelings of worth* come only when he can convince himself that he's better than someone else? What if *the only way he can build up his own ego* is by tearing someone else's ego down, or by scaring them or by humiliating them?"

Sammy chewed on his thumbnail for a few seconds. "Then I guess he would need some redirecting, repatterning, wouldn't he?"

"Can you imagine yourself as Casey? Close your eyes and try to put yourself in his place. He's probably been programmed by negative conditioning, and it doesn't matter at all whether it was environmental negative conditioning or parental negative conditioning or *self-inflicted negative conditioning. They all come out of the same container.*"

"Man, now I'm seeing Casey from a completely different perspective. In fact I'm seeing him like he's the old *me!* He's probably feeling that he's of no value or consequence, so why should he try to act *good* when he's positive he's *no good!* That's really a haunting, hurtful place to be in."

"It sounds hurtful."

"He probably feels that there's no way he can compete."

"*Why* can't he compete?"

"Because *he,* or society, or his parents have made him feel like he *can't!* He feels useless, worthless."

"Unlovely, unlovable?"

"Yeah. Like a failure, a bad kid."

"Is it possible that he can then justify himself by becoming the *best bad kid* around? That maybe even subconsciously, he tries to fill his ego needs through negativity, belittling, and hostility toward himself and others, and through crudeness, rudeness, loudness, and other socially unacceptable behaviors?"

"Yep. You got it. We're talking about Casey, plus probably me and all my sell-yourself-short mates of my olden days."

"Do you think maybe a better term than 'low self-esteem' might be 'low self-respect'?"

"Either way, attitude is everything. You long ago convinced me that people with self-respect and self-esteem don't need to bully or cut to feel important."

"I agree with you, Sammy the Significant! *Love and self-respect are this world's greatest equalizers.*"

Sammy grinned. "Ever were! Ever will be!"

107

We got up, stretched, had a drink, and ate some nuts and popcorn. "Want to take a little pop test?" I asked as I handed Sammy this sketch and a black felt-tipped pen.

He grinned.

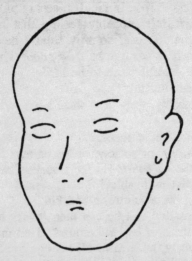

After Sammy had drawn strange hair, glasses, a mustache, a huge frown, and some moles with hair sticking out of them on the above sketch, I handed him the drawing on the next page and asked him to do with *it* what he had done with the first sketch.

"I can't do that."

"Why not?"

"Because it's Jesus."

"So?"

"It wouldn't be showing the proper re ... Oh, I get it now. You're trying to *graphically* teach me the *Respect Lesson*, the 'do unto others as ... as ... I would do unto Jesus.''

"Do you believe that?"

"Yes."

"Then maybe we'd better start trying a little harder to *live* what we believe, right?"

"Right! And with your help and Mom's and Dr. D.'s, I think I can ... NO! I *know* I not only can have more respect for myself, but I can help teach others to have more respect for themselves! Dr. D. is an ideal example of the respect thing."

"From what you've told me about him, I'm sure he is. It's too bad all kids don't have a few Dr. Davidsons in their lives."

"Oh, another thing I wanted to tell you about that Dr. D. and I have in common. When he was about four and a half and whining and bawling and lying on the floor and banging his head because he wanted to go outside and play, his grandma and mom found an old piano for him to take his frustrations out on. It was so out of tune that now every time we talk about it, he starts laughing. A lot of the strings were broken, so he'd have to hum the note that was silent if it was part the melody line. Anyway he said sometime he'll come over to my house and we'll have a piano duet jam since we can both play by ear as well as read music. Doesn't he sound like the dandiest dude of dudedom?''

"That he does! And I think I'm almost as glad as you are that he came to your school before you came back."

"I hate to think what might have happened to me if he hadn't."

"Then don't!"

"Don't what?"

"Don't think about negative things. Have you ever considered that you may not be able to keep an occasional disease-carrying fly out of your house, but you don't have to prop the door open so he and all his dirty, disease-carrying friends are invited in to swarm on your food and produce and reproduce till they—''

"Your allegory comes in loud and clear to me. But I still think it's a bummer that being smart and trying to learn is allowed to bring on abuse in some schools. Actually it was in mine to a degree before Dr. D. I remember lots of times I didn't do my best because I didn't want to be labeled 'computer head' or 'boodie brain.' Some of the kids would taunt that if your brain was too big for your 'boodie,' they'd have to whittle both down a bit. Or they'd say you were bringing up the learning curve so high it was making it hard on them, so they'd have to make it hard on you in return, which they did to a couple of kids. It was kind of gruesome seeing kids beat up right outside the schoolyard just because they were bright.''

"Didn't anyone go to the principal?"

"No one dared. We'd all heard there was a snitch in the office.''

"How did Dr. Davidson change things?"

"I heard he got rid of a lot of teachers and office staff and even some kitchen and custodial people, and that he really had to fight to do it.''

"Good for him! And for you! Now how about we . . .''

"I'm reading your body language . . . do a little more stirring around in *my* head.''

"Right. You don't know how wonderful it is working with someone like you where we are sort of in harmony in our thinking. People who aren't ready for change only compound their negative thoughts and attitudes and bring more discord and dissonance into their lives.''

"Don't include me in that group, lady. I am out! Out! *Out!* I want the old light and happiness and . . . I guess you could call it *MENTAL FREEDOM* from the black, squeezing-out-all-beautiful-and-good-things-in-reality, mental monsters. The blackness really does seem to have a life of its own, you know.''

"Therefore, poetic Sammy, I hope you've learned to be very, very compassionate toward any others you meet who might be suffering through their own menacing, monster depressions.''

"*Suffering through depression* is a good way to put it! I broke a couple of ribs skiing, and my arm Roller Blading, and I was in a car accident with my Uncle Milton, and in the drive-by shooting, but nothing ever hurt like the blackness inside my head and

111

heart and soul. It's like . . . if you haven't ever been there I hope you never, never, ever have to go.''

"All of us feel the colorless, emptiness of depression to one degree or another, at one point or another in our lives, Solemn Sammy, but usually those feelings are temporary and can be borne. Those of you who 'feed your problems,' knowingly or unknowingly, have a greater, blacker, sometimes permanent, or recurring, debilitating weight.''

Sammy tried to smile, but it was difficult. "At least I'm facing up to it now and scrambling my way out of the dung dungeon. I should get credit for that, shouldn't I?''

"You deserve and get all the credit in the world, all the stars in the sky.''

"Why doesn't everyone else just *do it,* too?''

"Some people have a physical chemical imbalance that sucks them down into a state so restricting that they find it difficult to eat, think, work, study, sometimes even to take care of their personal needs. They are imprisoned in their own kind of dark solitary confinement.''

"You mean they really *can't* get out?''

"Usually they can, once they start taking antidepressant drugs, tranquilizers, or whatever medication is needed for their particular problems.''

"I don't understand how that works.''

"It's not simple. Let me explain a little about Prozac. It is not a euphoriant or a sedative, and it doesn't have many of the side effects most of the drugs introduced in the late 1950s have.''

"And?''

"Okay, you want-to-know-it-all person, let me get my file. All right, Prozac comes in a little capsule containing about thirty-nine quintillion molecules of something called fluoxetine hydrochloride, which migrates to the brain when ingested. In the brain the molecules attach to nerve cells and prevent them from picking up serotonin, a neurotransmitter that passes electrical impulses from cell to cell.

"With less serotonin being picked up by the nerve cells, more of it remains in the brain, delivering small jolts of electricity from nerve to nerve, in a way sort of stimulating the voltage in the patient's head. Science doesn't, at this moment, understand precisely how this works, but the patient begins to find his/her way back into the light and freedom that once was his/hers. There are a *few* people who may need medication for the rest of their lives."

"I guess I'm pretty lucky to be me, aren't I?"

"Any way you look at it you're lucky to be you!"

"You think *some* of the people needing medical fixes could make the comeback without it?"

"By changing their attitudinal sets, their concepts about handling stress levels, and other things, *many* people certainly could improve their overall lifestyles and make their lives less complicated and threatening. Also by incorporating positive light therapy, positive exercise therapy, positive eating therapy, and all around enthusiastic, optimistic, reality therapy, they could help their bodies become more balanced in all areas, including chemically."

"That sounds like work!"

"It is work! But isn't anything worth having worth working for? And doesn't work seem like challenging fun if one has the proper attitude?"

"I didn't know you had to work at being happy."

"You don't! *After* you get into a pattern of putting the ingredients that cause happiness and balance into your life."

"How am I doing in that area?"

"Would you like to take home a little quiz to evaluate where you are?"

"Homework from a shrink?"

"From this one, yes! To me homework is imperative to change! At mental health seminars and conferences I sometimes hear about people who have gone to therapists for five, ten, or more years. They feel better when they are at the therapist's and may feel better for a while after they've left, but if they aren't *doing* some things themselves to make changes in their lives, change is not going to happen!"

"You're soooo right. Remember when I first came into your office? I didn't want to listen to or look at anything you had to offer. It was like you were spreading a fantastic emotional feast before me and I was *totally mentally anorexic.* No way would I have anything to do with it!"

"And there was no way in the world, at that time, that I could have forced you to!"

"Sorry about that."

"What has changed since then?"

"First of all MY 'TUDE! I now not only want to talk *and* listen, I want to pick your brains."

"You're saying you've seen the *positive* always-looking-for-the-good *Light of Life* that can shine within you even during the darkest storm on the darkest night."

"Yep. I think this time for sure I've conquered the darkness demons through my own kind of positive bright-white-light therapy. I'm making it a permanent part of myself, and I'm prepared to face a minor depression here and there because *my special light* will always *be turned on* in my heart or head or somewhere."

"That's deeply wonderful and mature, Sammy.

NOW you understand one of the greatest principles of life.''

"What?"

"That darkness *cannot* be taken into a lighted room or a lighted mind!"

"Are you telling me I'm finally getting my screwed-up self unscrewed?"

"I am! And you're getting there *fast!*"

"Wow! I'm solidly stoked!"

"You should be! That's why I'm giving you the SELF-EVALUATION ROAD MAP QUIZ to take home and work on."

"Road map?"

"You want to know if you're on the road to good mental health or mental illness, don't you?"

"It sounds scary."

"No way! Not for you! Answer the questions truthfully and thoughtfully in the first box. Every week answer them again in the second box, then the third box. When the boxes are full, erase all but the first answer and start over. You'll be delightfully surprised at how fast you'll grow and change once you become aware of what you are doing, or not doing, that can be detrimental to your mental health."

"I think I'm beginning to learn that in the future I will be mainly responsible for *making* both my good luck and my bad luck."

"And that it's not as much 'luck' in life as it is *ATTITUDE!* Have you ever heard the saying, 'IT'S YOUR *ATTITUDE* THAT DETERMINES YOUR *ALTITUDE*'?"

I handed him the quiz.

"That makes sense to me. See you."

SELF-EVALUATION
ROAD MAP TO MENTAL ILLNESS

Where do you want to go?
Where are you going?

Answer questions with a number from 0 to 10: 10 being often, 0 being never.

DESTINATION: MENTAL ILLNESS	WEEKS											
	1	2	3	4	5	6	7	8	9	10	11	12
1. I have low self-esteem												
2. I am hostile												
3. I am melancholy (sad)												
4. I seem detached from myself, others, life												
5. I am negative												
6. I am pessimistic												
7. I can't trust people or things												
8. I am fearful												
9. I am irritable												
10. I am not motivated												
11. I am critical												

DESTINATION: MENTAL ILLNESS	WEEKS											
	1	2	3	4	5	6	7	8	9	10	11	12
12. I am unappreciative												
13. I am indecisive												
14. I often feel inferior												
15. I feel guilty												
16. I feel unlovable												
17. I do not respect myself												
18. I feel hopeless												
19. I feel helpless												
20. I feel I am a burden												
21. I am impulsive (I want what I *want now!*)												
22. I am obsessive (I give my control to whatever)												
23. I am loud, crude, and rude												
24. I worry about my health												
25. I blame others												
26. I have suicidal impulses												
27. I hate—I'm angry												

Check your answers and YOU DECIDE if you are on the MENTAL ILLNESS ROAD. Do *you want* to change roads? *Can anyone else* change roads for you? *Should* you change roads? *Would* you be happier and mentally and physically healthier if you did? Are *you going* to change roads? If so, *when?* Is there a better time than *now?*

Retake the test in a week. You'll be surprised how much you'll have changed for the better.

However, only you can make the change!

SELF-EVALUATION
ROAD MAP TO MENTAL WELLNESS

Answer questions with a number from 0 to 10: 10 being often, 0 being never.

DESTINATION: MENTAL WELLNESS	WEEKS										
	1	2	3	4	5	6	7	8	9	10	11
1. I love and respect myself											
2. I love and respect others											
3. I feel happy and peaceful											
4. I enjoy being with others											
5. I enjoy being by myself											
6. I am positive											
7. I am optimistic											
8. I trust myself											
9. I trust others											
10. I know the difference between real and fanciful fears											
11. I am not easily irritated											
12. I am motivated											

	WEEKS										
	1	2	3	4	5	6	7	8	9	10	11
13. I enjoy my job, school, or whatever I am doing											
14. I am not critical											
15. I am appreciative											
16. I can make good decisions											
17. I do not feel inferior											
18. I do not feel hopeless											
19. I do not feel helpless											
20. I am not impulsive											
21. I am not obsessive											
22. I am not hostile											
23. "Down times" do not last more than two or three days											
24. Life is exciting, challenging, and fun											
25. I look forward to a happy, successful future											

Check your answers and YOU DECIDE if you are on the MENTAL WELLNESS ROAD.

Do *you want* to change some of your habits and thinking patterns? Do *you think* you should? Are *you going* to make the changes? If so, *when?* Is there a better time than *now?*

Check your answers once a week and if you are willing to *WORK* for change and positive growth there *will* be change and positive, happy, fulfilling, growth!

SUMMARY OF SESSION

Before Sammy's school started, he called two boys he grew up with and asked them to help him back. Dr. Davidson, the new principal, was once a gang member. He has sent all gang members to an alternative school. Sammy was given SELF-EVALUATION ROAD MAP QUIZ exercise papers so he could evaluate his own state.

Samuel Gordon Chart
Friday, September 9, 3:30 P.M.
————
Eighth Visit
SAMUEL (SAMMY) GORDON, 15 years old

NOTE: A message was left on the answering service voice mail. Sammy, sounding like he had been flattened by a steamroller, said he *had* to see me *right away!* I returned his call and suggested he come over as soon as possible. I never take lightly anyone's cries for help, particularly someone who is, or has been, suicidal.

"Who emptied your emotional tank?" I asked gently.

"It's a long, cold, black story."

"I can see and hear that you are hurting deeply. Let's tend to your wounds without wasting time."

Sammy crumpled into my La-Z-Boy chair and sobbed like a small child, his body contorted with suffering. For a long time I rubbed his head, neck, and shoulders. His muscles were taut, as tense as metal springs. Softly I started whispering to him. "Relax ... let go ... unwind ... release the pressure. You're safe and protected ... relax, relax." I began putting finger pressure on his shiatsu nerve centers.

"It's okay to cry, Sammy. It's even good to cry. It's pressure relieving and a natural response for relinquishing pain. Don't be ashamed or embarrassed. Be grateful that *you* have someone you trust enough to completely open your soul to and that you can cry around. You know I understand and care, don't you?"

Through his lessening sobs he sniffled, "Yeah."

It was some time before Sammy could talk. When he did the words tumbled out in such a jumble that they hardly made sense. Little by little the words began to string together into a semblance of sentences—agonizing, excruciating utterances that can only be completely understood by those who have suffered through truly deep depression.

"I wanted out," he said. "I wanted to do it! I felt I had to! I just didn't know how. My life isn't worth shit, nothing is. I'm certainly not worth shit to anybody, including myself."

"Whoa, boy. Relax and back up a bit. I know something has happened to *distort your thinking,* and that's all right. *Massively distorted thinking* has happened to many people long before you and will happen to many people long after you. Let's explore *what* got your thinking so out of whack. But first let me congratulate you.''

''Why would you want to congratulate me?''

''Because no matter how depressed you were or how distorted your thinking was, you *didn't* lose your control completely.''

''You just think I didn't.''

''No. You didn't do *it*. You might have thought about suicide, but you didn't try it—or did you?''

''No ...''

''And you came to me to sort of ...''

''Get my brains unscrambled?''

''You *could have* tried to run away from your new problem, whatever it is, couldn't you?''

''Yeah, but I am smart enough to know *now* that even if I did, no matter where I went, I'd take the problem with me.''

''See why I'm proud of you? You don't keep your brains in your pocket.''

''It seems I do most of the time.''

''Stop it! You are talking about a kid I admire and respect much more than he ever suspects! He's neat and he's cool and he's bright and he's good. So, he does goof up once in a while; we all do! It's part of being a member of the human race.''

''I'm dropping out of the race.''

''It's not that easy, friend. In the race of life you've got to expect some mountains and some alligator- and poisonous snake–filled swamps.''

''I'm too tired and mixed up for all that goody-goody, look-for-the-good crap.''

''Then I don't know what you're doing here. I'm the queen of goody-goody, and if you're happy, or at least content, to stay where you are, I can't stop you. Nobody can.''

A single big tear sneaked out of Sammy's right eye. "Please stop me! Please help me escape from the deep black, no-way-out pit I've dug myself into again. I don't know how I got from where I was to here. It happened sooo fast. Last time I did it, I let the black pain whop me. Then I tended it and nourished it and babied it until it grew bigger than I was. After a while, it literally became my dictator and slave master. This time the black pain came all at once like an avalanche, completely burying me, body and soul."

"Something must have triggered it, dear Sammy. Don't you honestly know what caused this self-destructive relapse?"

"I know," he said sadly.

"Do you want to talk about it?"

His head fell down on his chest, and his body tightened.

"Do you think you *should* talk about it?"

Silence.

"Is it possible you *must* talk about it before you can relieve the pain and stress and find the secret passage out of the darkness?"

He sighed so deeply that it seemed to come from his toes. "I can't! Well, maybe I can. I'll do whatever *you want*."

"It doesn't work that way, Sammy. Remember, I can't take responsibility for your life. *You* must *want to do* whatever it is you *should do!*"

"There isn't any other way?"

"There is no other way! All of us have to accept the consequences for each of our actions: *Positive rewards for positive actions and negative penalties for negative actions*. Does that compute?"

"Yeah."

124

"So? What was the action or thought, or whatever, that caused you to again dredge up your old rotting garbage and willfully wallow in it?"

"How did you know I'd done that?"

"It was easy. You were emotionally reeking with the stench of all your old fetid sewage."

"Looks like the first time I had to face up to a consequence, I dived right back into the old black septic tank I'd just managed to climb out of, doesn't it?"

"And was it wise?"

"No. But I didn't know what to do. I just wanted to escape from the humiliation, the embarrassment . . . the pain."

"Did you?"

"Hardly! Instead of escaping from all of it I compounded it a hundred million, zillion times."

"Smart move?"

"Dumb move! One of my dumbest! Of all the stupid things I've ever done . . . the super stupidest!"

"Want to vent exactly what happened?"

"Well, it had been a while since I'd seen you, and I was feeling pretty good about myself and everything else. I'd apologized to all my old teachers, and Dr. Davidson and I were pretty tight, and Marv and Tommy and I were solid. I really thought I was making it big time and then . . . it'll probably seem like a little thing to you."

"Not if it's big to you."

"I'd seen Harmony in the halls a few times, and it was like I was being butchered inside. I wanted so much to do something . . . fall at her feet and grovel for her forgiveness . . . hold her close like I'd never let her go . . . kidnap her . . . all sorts of crazy things ran through my mind. I knew sometime I'd have to face her. I dreaded it in a way, but I couldn't wait for it just as much.'' Sammy stopped for a long time and agonized.

"Tuesday, as I was coming out of Mrs. Procter's class, I saw Mo walking down the hall looking like springtime and flowers and sunshine and all the other good things in life rolled up together in the most beautiful package in the world. I loved her so much I couldn't breathe. She was like something spiritual, an angel or something coming toward me.

"Then suddenly my head almost collapsed with the unbelievable memory of the day under the bleachers when, for absolutely no reason except pent-up hostility, I'd hit her, not once, but three times, hard. My right hand felt black and evil. I wanted to cut it off to show how mistaken I'd been and how sorry I was. Then I recalled every good thing that had ever happened between me and her. I don't know how so much stuff could pass through my mind in such a short time.

"I was about ready to smile when Chick Laddel, the guy the gang used to call 'Chicken Little,' rounded the corner and put his arm possessively around her. 'Glad you're back, Sammy,' he said, in a way that seemed sincere. He turned to Mo. 'Aren't we glad he's back, babe?' Mo looked right through me as though I wasn't even there. 'Who? Where? I don't see anybody, anybody at all.' She put her arm tightly through his and pulled him away.''

"How painful that must have been.''

"It was like the bottom dropped out of my world right there, and I was sucked down into my old black, airless hole in one quick swoosh, down into eternal darkness. All the new lightness and the brightness were zapped, and my old bitter past entrapped me completely, strangling me in its black, musty, dirty, escape-proof net. I turned and walked out of school, and went home to my room, where I've stayed for the past few days, swallowed up by blackness and hostility and evil. Each feeding the other and multiplying and enlarging and devouring my body and my soul and my mind.

"Mom thought I had the flu, and I gladly took anything and everything she gave me, looking for any kind of relief at all. I wished like everything that I had done the deed when I had had the chance. Mom had a little pistol hidden on the top shelf in her closet, but I couldn't find where she had put the clip. I looked in the medicine cabinet, but there wasn't anything there that would do the job. The black pain was excruciating."

"What else might you have done about it?"

"Nothing. I was so defeated and deflated, I . . ."

"Think carefully and slowly now. At that time *what were you* doing?"

"I was . . . giving complete control of my thinking to . . ."

"To what?"

"To all the *NEGATIVE POWERS* that surrounded me."

"They had forcefully overcome you or *YOU* had willingly handed over to them *your* remote control power?"

"I'm such a ratty, bratty boob tube."

"No! No, you're just a normal person who hasn't quite learned the secret of *staying in charge* of your life! Have you noticed that once you let a negative in, *it* becomes magnetic and attracts multitudes of other negatives which become even bigger and stronger and blacker and more malignant and cannibalistic? And the negatives come from every conceivable direction: up, down, north, south, east, west, over, under, and sideways."

"And it seems all the negatives a person has kept hidden or semicontrolled inside explode out as well."

"*That* is right on! Once you even move toward the NEGATIVITY TRAP—"

Sammy interrupted. "Everything bad in the universe, both inside and outside, comes tumbling down around you. But what could I have done, both times when it seemed the world literally did come crashing in on my head?"

"Each of us should, actually *must*, have an *enormous retaliating positive arsenal* safely tucked away in some remote place in our brains so that no negative mental monster will ever have the slightest chance of *taking over!* You've heard the old saying, 'you can't keep birds from flying over your head, but you *can* keep them from making nests in your hair.' That's exactly the way it is with negatives."

"Sounds good, but at this point I feel like dead meat."

I pinched his arm. "Oh, no, you're not. See?"

Sammy winced and let out a little squeak. "Okay, so the experience didn't kill me!" He became very serious. "But it did completely cripple and defeat me emotionally." He hesitated for a few seconds. "Now *you're* going to say, What could *I* have done about it, right?"

"Probably. What could you, what should you, have done immediately after the incident?"

"Well, I could have called you."

"Yes, you know very well that you can call me any hour of the day or night. Or?"

"I could have gone home and sat under my relighting-myself bright-light, because believe me, at that time every light in my life had gone out. I'd seen the look on Mo's face. I knew she knew she'd mortally wounded me, and she liked it!''

"Wait a minute. Let's go over that one more time. Are you trying to *justify putting the responsibility for your descent into depression on Mo?*"

"Of course not! It's just that she'd *wanted* to humiliate me, hurt me, break me, so ... Whoa ... I can feel the enemy attacking. Where's my arsenal? Okay, *only positives* can defeat negatives and drive away the darkness. POSITIVES! POSITIVES! POSITIVES! Mo was totally innocent! I was the one who hit her! I was the one who became hostile and impossible to be with. I was the jerk, the pit, the irresponsible ...''

"Hey, wait a minute. Are you in some irrational way trying to rationalize that *negatives used on yourself* don't count?''

"Umm, I guess I was trying to do that, wasn't I? I need you around all the time to set me straight.''

"No, you don't! Tell me what you really need.''

"To have more confidence in myself and my own judgments and to take a little more time and thought about what I think and say before I say and do!''

"Have you ever tried talking to yourself?''

"No, way! I used to see my grandpa do it, and old men who sit on park benches.''

"Don't laugh. Discussing things rationally with yourself can be therapeutic. If you had started a comprehensive conversation with yourself, like you and I have, you could have come to practically the same conclusions we came to.''

"Is that really true?''

"Yes. It's really true.''

"Are you saying that if I'd gone home after the Mo incident and I'd, say, sat under my bright-white-light and I'd tried to rationally and verbally sort things out, that I could have kept myself, through my own sort of self-therapy, from falling into the deep, black, funky pit that I'd dug and redug for myself?"

"Almost surely! It's better to talk to someone else if you can: your family, a friend, someone on a crisis hot line, a counselor, whatever. But if you can't contact anyone else, make mental and verbal contact with yourself. We human beings are all a lot smarter and deeper than we give ourselves credit for being."

"It's strange to think that I might have kept myself out of the depression party I invited all my old negative, mental monster friends to, and maybe not been tempted to go the suicide route. But that wouldn't have helped me figure out how I could have handled the Mo thing."

"You were maybe expecting *me* to do that?"

He halfheartedly laughed. "No, knowing you, I know *you're* expecting *me* to do it by my poor, little, innocent, crushed, hurting self."

"Poor baby."

"*Big baby!* But I wouldn't admit that to anyone else in the world if my life depended on it."

"You life *doesn't* depend on it, so what might you do to get yourself out of the black corner you have painted yourself into?"

"I could blow out ..."

"That's *not* acceptable to *you*, I hope."

"No. Maybe I could beat up on Chicken Little."

"What would that get you?"

"A few bangs and bruises and maybe I'd release some hostility."

"Would it change anything or solve anything?"

"No, and even the thought is kind of childish. Let's see, I could phone Mo, but I'm sure she'd hang up on me. Maybe I could have my mom talk to her mom. Oops! That idea is straight out of the cracker crock. I guess I could write her ... maybe a long, long letter telling her the absolute truth about how I used to feel about things and then how I went through the dark times and now how I want so very, very, very much to be forgiven and to start over, just as friends. I don't deserve to be more than a friend because how could she possibly trust me after ... you know. Do you think that might work?"

"Do you think it might?"

"Maybe. At least it would clear my conscience a little and make me feel better in that regard. In fact, I feel a lot better just having talked it over with you. I mean myself! I'm going to try that crisis hot line thing sometime, too, to see if it works, and I may even try talking to my mom." He grinned. "It's a sure thing she'd be nicer to me than you are sometimes."

"You mean the times when I make *you* take responsibility for your own mistakes, and have *you* make your own good decisions?"

"When did I ever do the good decision part?"

"Super Sam, stop beating up on yourself! Remember, you've got to be your own best friend, coach, mentor, advisor, therapist, minister, promoter, agent, ego-inflater, booster, cheerleader, and everything else that is up-building and positive, all the things that will make *YOU* your best *YOU!*"

"That sounds kind of egotistical and vain."

"Or does it sound like you want to make the best and happiest of yourself so that you can, in turn, help others make the best and happiest of themselves?"

"Okay, so I'm a good guy, a bright guy, a guy who has made some major mistakes, but one that desperately wants to start over, with a new 'tude, a POS 'TUDE ALL THE WAY! ALL THE TIME! Does that satisfy you?"

"It satisfies me if it satisfies you! All I want is for you to be physically, mentally, emotionally, and spiritually healthy and well balanced."

Sammy smiled lamely. "You're sure you don't want me to be translated, too?"

I gave him a hard noogie. "No. But I do think sometime you should unload your 'beginning thing.' "

"I intend to do that—next never-day! But thanks for seeing me in a hurry. I think I've got at least Plan A sort of lined up in my mind. I really do appreciate you."

"Don't appreciate me. Appreciate the girl who had your appointment. When I called and told her you, no name, had a *right now problem* and that you were in an extremely hurtful situation, she gladly gave up her time, remembering when she had been in a like place herself."

"I'm sorry."

"You needn't be. It was good for her. Part of her healing. She was given the pleasure of helping someone else to heal himself, and that puts a different spin on it for both of you."

"Well, thank her and think luck to me."

"I'd rather think *pos thoughts* for you."

"Pos thoughts for you, too. Bye."

I raised my hand to wave good-bye and bit my lip, I wanted so much to ask him to call and let me know what happened.

Sammy looked at me knowingly. We were kindred

132

spirits, as all people would be if they would just allow it.

"I know what you're thinking, brain unscrambler. You want me to let you know what happens."

"I'm trapped. The student has now become the all-knowing teacher. The client has become the therapist."

He sighed deeply. "I wish."

I *wished* all my clients could be as intuitive and open and anxious to learn and change and heal themselves. If he knew the resistance that the girl who had given up her time had encountered along her way back, he probably would have appreciated her magnanimous gesture a hundred times more.

As Sammy left I handed him my standard exercise on Distorted Thinking.

DISTORTED THINKING EVALUATION

QUESTION: How can I tell when my
thoughts are distorted?
ANSWER: *When you sense they are negative.*

Everyone has negative *things* happen in their lives,
but *the mentally healthy person looks for positive
solutions, positive coping skills, and even positive
standing stills!* The Alcoholics Anonymous' Serenity
Creed is an inspired example of the above.

God grant me the serenity to accept the things I
cannot change, the courage to change the things I
can, and the wisdom to know the difference.

Grade yourself from A to F on the following test.

Retake the test once a week, grading yourself each
time. You'll love watching your positive progression!

GRADE (WEEKS 1 to 4)

				1. I felt discouraged and I
				I should have
				2. Someone irritated me and I
				I should have
				3. Someone didn't give me the attention I needed so I
				I should have
				4. The wind blew my new ? into the mud and I
				I should have

				5. Someone in authority told me what to do and I
				I should have
				6. I felt jealous and I
				I should have
				7. My self-esteem was low so I
				I should have
				8. I felt guilty and I
				I should have
				9. I felt sad and I
				I should have
				10. I felt mad and I
				I should have
				11. I felt a suicidal thought and I
				I should have

Write your own list of things that "bug" you, hurt you, or in other ways make you feel *negative*. This is an effective and quick way to heighten your awareness regarding incidents that *can* distort your thinking and build up negatives like pebbles in your pack until they, the little things, as well as the big things, *can* weigh you down into the blackest of all black pits of depression. Never allow yourself to forget that the way to *negate* a *negative thought* or *action* is to NEUTRALIZE IT WITH A BRIGHT-WHITE-LIGHT *POSITIVE* THOUGHT OR ACTION!

The key to having good mental health and staying in control is:

- as old as dirt
- as simple and as warming as sunshine
- as comforting as love
- and as eternal as *positivity*

Positivity is taught in the Bible, the Koran, the Torah, the teachings of Buddha and Confucius in China, Vishnu and others in India, and throughout most cultures and religions. The premise is simple, "For as he *thinketh* in his (her) heart, so is he (she)." (Proverbs 23:7)

SUMMARY OF SESSION

Sammy faced his self-imposed self-destructive relapse regarding Harmony (Mo). He is beginning to understand the NEGATIVE TRAP that is always out there.

Samuel Gordon Chart
Saturday night, September 10, 10:32 P.M.
***

Telephone Conversation
SAMUEL (SAMMY) GORDON, 15 years old

Sammy Gordon called. I had been asleep, but the moment I heard his voice I was as alert as it is possible for a person to be. After his first "hello" I wanted to ask what happened? Instead I put on my professional therapist's demeanor and listened as he said that things between him and Mo were "cool," but that he wanted to see me soon. Remembering that I was going out of town on Monday, I suggested maybe we could have a "freebie" lunch session. I'd meet him in the park just blocks from his house and we'd pick up a couple of hot dogs from the vendor.

.

Samuel Gordon Chart
Sunday, September 11, noon
———————

Freebie Lunch Session in the park
Ninth Visit
SAMUEL (SAMMY) GORDON, 15 years old

"Hi, Wow, you sprang for puppy dogs and everything. Thanks, good buddy."

"Thank you."

"For what?"

"For *being you!* Connecting with kids like you who are willing to work at changing their lives, is the greatest joy and reward any mental health professional can receive."

"You're prejudiced because I've got green eyes like yours."

"No."

"Okay, guess you just casually came to hear about Mo."

"*You* and Mo."

"Well, when I got home from seeing you on Friday I spent hours writing and rewriting and rewriting a letter to her. I didn't tell her every detail about how I'd gotten off track in the *first place*, just how lost and confused and unstrung and upset and scram-

137

bled I'd become after that. How it had made me feel like an outcast from my own race, like a subspecies or something. How, after that, I couldn't relate to Mom and the girls, or myself, or anyone, or anything, even her. I told her how horrifically and eternally sorry I was for the time under the bleachers, and that I'd understand if she could never forgive me. I told her how lonely and dark and unprotected and unlovely and unloved I'd felt in that nonworld, and how I'd been irresistibly drawn to the gang because I felt they'd take me in when nobody else would, or could. I told her I often felt that *most* of the guys in the gang felt like I did, that the only way to survive was through physicalness. They didn't know any other way, and *I had allowed myself to forget* all the other ways."

Sammy stopped long enough to scarf down a hot dog, then continued his story, almost in a trance. "It was after midnight when I finally finished the letter and sneaked it up to her house and slipped it through the mail slot in the front door. My heart was pounding so hard that I could feel the blood roaring in my ears and in my head. It was hammering in my chest like a jackhammer. I wondered for a minute if I was going to have a heart attack on her front walk, and the medics and police would come with their sirens screaming, and everybody would either feel sorry for me as anything or want to drag off my carcass and throw it with good riddance into the Dumpster."

"Dear, dear, Samuel Gordon. How deeply you must have hurt."

He seemed to ignore me, or perhaps he was so deep into his experience that he actually didn't hear me.

"I had always gotten good grades in English; now I worried and agonized about my spelling and punctuation and syntax and stuff that was totally irrelevant. The night was endless. I felt I was caught in some kind of time warp that just stayed in place."

"But you did get out of it. You're here."

"Yeah, eventually. After eons and eternities and infinities, the phone rang."

He stopped and sucked at his Coke so slowly that I couldn't stand it.

"And?"

"It was her, Mo! I thought I was hallucinating or whatever it is you do when you don't hear right. Then she started to cry, and as her tears ran through the phone wires I felt like they were drowning me, too, or maybe *they* were my own tears at that point. She said she'd read every word of my letter four or five times, and she didn't know when she'd ever felt so compassionate and empathetic in her life. I woke Mom up and asked her if we could have Mo over for breakfast.

"Mom was as happy as I was, and she woke the girls and all three of them started chirping around the house like it was Christmas or something. It's really funny, maybe even scary how many people are there to help you when you're honestly trying to turn your life around. For one moment I felt how *unworthy* I was, then I made one of the firmest commitments I've ever made in my life. I would live worthy of all the blessings that had ever been, and would ever be, given to me. It made me feel so good that . . . I dunno."

"That you began chirping, too?"

"Yes, I guess. And I got a million things to do,

like go see Mo at two-thirty, but I just had to tell you."

"You're a good, strong, brilliant, straight-thinking young man. You're to be admired, Sammy Gordon, and don't you ever forget it!"

He grinned and sprinted off down the street. After a few steps he stopped and yelled, "I didn't read your *Distorted Thinking* stuff, but I'm going to soon. Promise!"

I couldn't help wondering how much his reaction to "the Mo thing" would have changed if he *had* read the "Distorted Thinking stuff" *before his* distorted thinking episode.

Samuel Gordon Chart
Wednesday, September 21, 9 P.M.

Telephone Conversation
SAMUEL (SAMMY) GORDON, 15 years old

Sammy telephoned. I could immediately tell by his voice that something was way off track. This time he didn't seem angry, frustrated, or depressed, but rather completely unemotional, like he had turned *all* his feelings off completely. I interrupted to ask if I could record our conversation so that he could listen to it later and perhaps consider our discussion from a different perspective. He consented in the same colorless, nobody-home monotone he had been using, and I turned the machine on.

"What's happening, Sammy?"

"As though I don't have enough to handle, Lance has started *really* boogering up my life."

"Lance? Your father?"

"He's been writing, phoning, sending telegrams and . . . right now I simply can't handle *his* nuttiness on top of my own. He just called *four times!*"

"What does he say?"

"I don't know. I just hang up the phone like I tear up his letters and stuff."

"Oh."

"He even had the guts to send me his old original Fats Waller music chart that he knew I'd always coveted."

"What did you do about that?"

"I sent it back with a message scribbled across the top of the package: RECEIVER UNKNOWN TO YOU."

"How did that make you feel?"

"I feel nuthin'! It's like he and I are protoplasm or something. How can protoplasm be expected to feel anything?"

"Does your mom know about this?"

"Yeah, he's been annoying her, too, with his stupid stuff."

"What does she want to do . . . want you to do?"

"I don't know. I won't let her talk. I won't listen. I don't want to hear."

"Did you hear what you just said?"

He hesitated for a few seconds. "You mean about the . . . I don't want to hear?"

"Yes."

"Well, it's true. I want him to just . . . drop dead . . . leave me . . . leave us alone."

"Do you mean that literally?"

"Absolutely!"

"Absolutely?"

Well, maybe not absolutely. I just want him to go away . . . stay out of our lives! I was just beginning to think I was getting all my gonzos together and feeling pretty much like the old me and then this came up."

"What came up?"

"Mom's insisting that I talk to him."

"And?"

"And no way am I going to let that drop-us-on-our heads, retard bastard . . . sorry. Anyway, no way am I going to let . . . him . . . into my life again! He's too big a part of the shit I'm just shuffling out of. He made his choice! He's outta my life . . . gone . . . disappeared . . . evaporated . . . vanished . . . passed, I WISH!"

"It sounds like you're facing quite a challenge."

"Yeah."

"Do you think it might be easier to find a solution for the problem than just to stand there and let it keep pounding on your head?"

"Sure it would be, if there was a solution."

I sat quietly for a few seconds, happy that Sammy had turned more than his pilot light on.

"There's gotta be some way out!"

"Ummmm." I wanted Sammy to discover his own way out.

"Well I could . . . I don't know. I just know I can't talk to him."

"Can't?"

He started venting his anger on me. "You think it would be so easy! You don't understand that he would just pulverize me, bury me in that black, stinking hellhole I'm just getting out of, so deep I'd never get out again, ever! I don't know why in hell I ever called you."

"Because you know I *care* about you and can help, if you'll let me."

Sammy started crying. Deep, wracking, rocky, dry sobs that shuddered through the phone line and into my ear. "I thought I was getting it together. I really did. Now I'm right back ..."

"No, you're not, dear Sammy. Believe me I've been *here* before with many other kids, and there *will be* an honorable, happy way out."

"I hope you're right." He thought for a while. "I know you're right! I got lost in the canyon once when I was a little kid, and I didn't think I'd ever get out, especially when it got dark and I heard every scary sound that had ever been barked or growled or woofed or whistled or hooted by any beast or fowl that had ever been created."

"*Did* you get out, that's the question."

"Yes, I did, and I did it all by my tiny little self-assertive self, well almost by myself. Actually one of the track dogs found me and took me back."

"Is *this* more scary and difficult than that?"

"Every bit *as*! But you're not going to say what I want you to say, are you?"

"Probably not, if you think I'm not."

"At times like this when you're so mean to me, I wonder what we're paying you for." He sounded embarrassed. "That's a joke, lady."

"Okay, I'm laughing."

"Well, let's see, since I have to do all the work. What about if we sent all the bastards in my life a one-way ticket to Somalia?"

"I suppose you and I will print the money for the multitude's tickets?"

"Now you're laughing *at* me."

"No, I'm laughing with you."

"I guess that's better than crying."

"Yeah, lots."

"Mom really wants me to talk to him."

"Have you considered it?"

"Do you think I could handle it?"

"You know I *know* you can!"

"But only if it's just me and him and you!"

"Sounds certified sane to me."

"And Mom, don't you think we should have Mom?"

"I do, if you do."

"You're such a wuss. You make me do all the work and hard thinking and putting together, and you know all along what you're pushing me into, don't you?"

"Yep, sometimes."

"Well ... okay. If you insist, I'll have Mom call and tell him to meet us at your place. When?"

"Do you want it to be soon?"

"The sooner the better. It's going to be a hairy, scary encounter."

I looked at my calendar. "Do you think he can make it late this Friday the twenty-third or early Saturday the twenty-fourth?"

"Part of me hopes *he* can't."

"Part of you hopes he can too, so you can get this challenge over with, right?"

"Nope. Well, yep. I guess it has to be done sometime. Actually I can't wait to get it over with so I can get on with my life."

"Good for you! Call me if those dates aren't feasible. I'll try to make time, *anytime* for you."

"You're looking forward to seeing me crunched and smashed and mashed and bashed aren't you?"

"Not."

"I know you're *not*. That's the only reason I can say it. Keep your fingers crossed."

"It's not going to be nearly as bad as you may think, Sammy."

"If you say so! I'll try to hang on to that thought, and don't worry about me. I'm going to go sit under the light therapy lamp and relax ... relax ... relax. Like you say, 'Relax ... rest ... refresh ...' I'll pretend I'm in a buttercup-covered meadow with a little trout stream gurgling by, and I'll listen to the pos things we've discussed on the tapes I've brought home and I'll start, RIGHT NOW, putting back into my life all the ingredients that will make me happy and healthy and whole."

"Sounds good to me, therapist's pet. See ya soon."

Sammy's voice tightened into a metallic sound. "But what I honestly, really need is ... could you ... would you ..."

"When?"

"I dunno ... maybe I don't really need you ... I'm just being ..."

"What about early tomorrow morning before anyone else gets up?"

"How come you're so good to me?"

" 'Cause, believe me, YOU'RE WORTH IT!"

"Thanks much. See ya in the A.M."

PHONE CALL SUMMARY

Sammy phoned Wednesday night, September 21, at 9:00 P.M.

His father, Lance, insists on seeing him. We made an appointment for tomorrow morning at 7:00 A.M.

Tenth Visit
SAMUEL (SAMMY) GORDON, 15 years old

"Hi, Sammy."

"Hi." He was so intense he appeared almost ready to fragment.

"You look like you need a friend to vent on."

"You mean dump on?"

"I mean dump on."

Sammy cringed. His pain seemed excruciating, physically as well as mentally. "I've got to do something! That loser Lance is trying to stir up the whole hellhole of my past. I don't need that! Every bad thing that's ever happened since creation has come flooding back, overwhelming me, undermining me. He's opened up the Pandora's box that I swore I'd never let be reopened." Sammy sniffed and wiped his nose on the back of his hand. "Why doesn't the bastard sadist just leave us alone? He's already dumped us ... started my life on the road to ruination."

I gripped his shaking hands tightly. "No, he hasn't. He can't! Because *you* won't let him! We won't let him!"

Sammy seemed to have drifted out to another time, another dimension. "It wasn't just him—it was—oh how I hate that asshole's guts. I'll never forgive him for worlds without end. He's beaming up hate at me from Hell every minute of every day and I'm beaming hate down to him in Hell."

146

"Hey. Wait a minute, Sammy. You can't control what others do with their energy even if they waste it on something as detrimental as hate. I thought you were going for more positive things now."

"I wish I could, but I can't, and I can't run away anymore, either." He curled up into a pathetic ball in the corner of his chair.

"I think you can face anything now, Sammy. In fact, maybe *now* is the time when you've *got* to face it. I'll help you. Promise, I'll help you! You simply cannot run from *him* anymore."

"I guess it has been pretty damn stupid of me to think I could make something that bad go away by itself, hasn't it?"

"Maybe, but it's *more* than pretty bright for you to now decide to do what you ought to do."

"Okay. Ready . . . set . . . go."

"First, I should *know for sure* who *he* is so that we can better treat all your hostility and negative feelings in a get-rid-of, get-better way.

"It was . . . it was the male who . . . fertilized my mom's egg they called Eggbert."

"You mean your father?"

"I have a nightmare almost every night about that lunatic degenerate. I want to vomit up all his genes that are in my body and throw them on the highway with the rest of the rotten roadkill."

"I know it's not easy or pleasant, Sammy, but it would help me and make the solution to your dilemma simpler if you could tell me the details."

He looked desperate.

"Would it make it easier if you held your nose, like I'm sure you did when you were a little kid and had to swallow some kind of medicine that you didn't think could be swallowed?"

The desperate look dissipated. It was replaced with a forced, mean, little boy grin. "Okay, stand back while I puke it up."

"Standing back, sir."

Sammy started talking. He spoke like someone reading a script. "Well, the first two days of Christmas vacation when I was with . . . Lance."

"Your dad?"

"Yeah. Everything seemed cool as usual. Then one night I couldn't sleep, and I crept downstairs to see what was in the fridge . . ."

"And?"

"I could hear Lance and a couple of the guys from the office in the den. I didn't want to disturb them, so I started to turn back but something sounded . . . or felt . . . I dunno, kind of funny, so I stopped and peeked through a plant that stands in the hall." Sammy gasped and blew his nose vigorously. "They were getting ready to snort cocaine. I'd never seen anyone doing it for real but, of course, I'd seen it done on TV and in the movies." Sammy's voice started shaking, and he held onto his chair as though it were a lifeline of some sort.

"I couldn't move. I just crouched there, watching them acting and talking stupid. Mom had always taught me about *bad consequences for bad actions and terrible consequences for terrible actions*. I was thoroughly confused. Could this be my old man? I'd experimented, but basically my four close friends and I had tried very hard to think seriously about drugs, alcohol, and sex. Now these crazy, depraved old men were glorifying all three. It was sick! Sick and sickening! In their stupid, stoned condition they weren't even men anymore. They were mindless, slippery, slimy, drooling nonhumanoid animals slumped on the couch. I wanted to throw up or disintegrate or something. I couldn't stand it. It was like physical pain, only worse, because it was inside my head and heart and soul, too.''

I rolled my chair close to Sammy's and clasped his hands empathetically. He squeezed back so hard I winced.

He continued, "Can you imagine what that did to a kid who had committed to stay straight? Well, kind of straight. It really about did me in right there. Anyway, after a few minutes I got my gonzos together and crept back upstairs, but I could have stomped up or fallen down and broken my neck, and they wouldn't have noticed or cared.''

"That must have been a horrifying and hurtful experience, Sammy.''

"It was, and it seemed like at that very moment all the lights in my mind turned off. I know that sounds crazy, but that's what really happened. I've lived in a gray cold world every moment since, a grey cold world with no music and no sunshine. It's depressing and demented . . . and I'm soooo alone. Even in the middle of a crowd of people I'm . . . like alone on an always-dark, always-will-be-dark, island.''

"Don't worry about that, Sammy. Most people who are carrying heavy negative burdens feel that their lights have gone out, or at least dimmed perceptibly.''

"Yeah, we've talked about how defeat and negativism drowns out sunshine, and I believe it . . . I know it! But I'm still all covered with dark inside.''

"Does that mean you've *absolutely got to expel* every bit of the darkness you've been hoarding?''

"For sure.''

"So? Do you feel like going on?"

"Yeah, I guess. It might feel good to dump it once and for all, to get the taste of it out of my mouth and the stench and pain of it out of my all-over-body-and-soul! Well ... I honestly don't know how this next stuff happened. I was repulsed and disgusted by watching Lance get stoned, and yet after he'd gone to the office the next day to pick up some things, I carefully pulled out his stash from the secret place among his books, actually a hollow block which looked like a shelf support. My hands were trembling so hard I could hardly get the block out and slide down the dummy back. As I started to put a little line of the white stuff on the coffee table, I dropped the box. Slowly the powder disappeared into the plush white carpeting. At that point I didn't care! I wanted to hurt *him*. He'd have to rush me off to the hospital, crying and sobbing and begging for my forgiveness and swearing he'd get his life cleaned up."

Sammy closed down and sat in a catatonic state until I began gently rubbing his shoulders, arms, and neck. Within a short time he had loosened up, so I whispered, "You can tell me the rest now, Sammy, if you'd like to. Don't you think it will be a great relief to *you* both mentally and physically when you regurgitate every bit of the fetid garbage you've been carrying around for so long?"

He nodded slightly and started talking again in the same low, lifeless monotone. "While I was still stoned out of my box, Lance came home and caught me. He beat on me and screamed at me and cursed me. In between bouts, he tried to brush up what seemed to be his most precious possession in the world from the carpet. It didn't work. The shit just sank deeper and deeper into the fibers, and Dad got crazy madder and madder. Finally he dragged me to my feet and yanked me up the stairs to my room, not really my room, his study. Nothing was mine in that mental and physical torture chamber, certainly not his caring concern or love.

"I kept slipping in and out of reality and consciousness. For one second I was afraid I was going to die, then I didn't care because it wasn't like in the movies, where the good guy helps the dumb guy and walks him around and puts cold towels on his head and begs him to come back and stuff. I remember trying to say, 'Just leave me alone. I'll die and get out of your way like you want me to, like you've probably always wanted me to,' but the words came out garbled and meaningless, and Lance kept on screaming and roaring and condemning.

"In some ways it was like an old black-and-white horror movie happening to someone else, actually a strange, mutant, ugly, burdensome kid who wasn't worth spit, to say nothing of *shit*. I'd been afraid I wasn't going to live, then I started becoming afraid *I would!* His hammering went on and on and on as he did and said everything odious that could be said or done to a helpless kid, and I cared less and less and less.

"I don't know how much later my mind started working again. Slowly I figured out what had happened, how much the evil person who was supposed to be my father had dehumanized me, degraded me, demoralized me. What a depraved degenerate he was, and I'd probably grow up to be just like him. I vowed to fool fate. I'd snuff myself! It seemed the only way out! I hurt so much that I remember looking down at my crumpled body and thinking I must be either

151

broken or bleeding in every bone and molecule. I was surprised that I wasn't. I kept asking myself over and over what kind of a degenerate in the whole world would or could love his shit more than he loved his own son?

"As soon as I was able to I found my wallet and sneaked out the fire escape. My only wish was to go home. Home to my mom, who cared about me and loved me. Or did she really? Did anybody? Could they? I probably had all my dad's dud genes, and I'd turn out exactly like him, but at least, I promised myself, I wouldn't have any kids to pass the degenerate crap on to." Sammy suddenly stopped talking. He looked both physically and emotionally exhausted.

"Want to take time out for a drink?"

"I need something. The more caffeine in it the better." He wheezed. "I thought you said puking up the gut-and-brain-and-heart-rot would make me feel better."

"I promise you it will! As soon as you get all the bad and sad garbage out of your body, you can replace the black haunting negatives with bright, wholesome, peace and happiness-giving positives."

He took a deep, noisy swig of Pepsi. "I hope you're right. I gotta count on your being right! It seems there's no other out for me. I wanted to dump everything, and yet, like I said before, I didn't want to. Either way it's painful."

"There doesn't seem to be a kind, gentle, slower, easier, way."

"I remember once when I broke a couple of ribs skiing, and after they healed the nurse started taking off the heavy tape inch by inch until I just screamed at her to take the damn thing off in one horrible yank instead of slowly and forever torturing me."

"Sometimes that's best."

"Well, in the weeks after the 'Lance thing' it wasn't a matter of whether I wanted to commit suicide, it was just a matter of how I was going to do it. In fact it was exciting in a way, imagining myself pulled down slowly under the black soft water after I'd jumped off the bridge, or just drifting off peacefully into eternal nothingness after I'd overdosed on something, or watching my family lower the casket into the ground with everybody, including the kids at school, crying and feeling sorry for me and ashamed of how they'd treated me."

"Had the kids at school and your family, excluding your father, really treated you that badly?"

"No, but at that time, in my black rage, I thought they had, which hurt just as much as if they really had."

"Oh, Sammy, you're *so wise* to understand now the concept that sometimes when we're being sucked down into a cold dark funk we *see everything* in relation to how we see ourselves at *that* particular moment."

"That's strange and true, isn't it? Actually, I hadn't really thought about it before, but the concept is scary, probably dangerous."

"More potentially dangerous and "self-destructive" than most people realize, except *you*, smart kid."

"Next time something like that happens, if there ever is a next time, and I pray there never will be, I'll talk to someone before I let it take over my whole existence—definitely before I accept suicide as 'the only way out.' "

"Will that be easy or pleasant?"

"Probably not, but I don't want the whatever it is

153

to grow like *Jack's* bean stalk either. Do you remember that story?"

"Of course I do. It was one of my favorites, except for the big, scary giant at the top."

"You know that's kind of like this whole 'Lance thing.' It started, and I let it grow. I actually knew how poisonous it was, still I nourished it by transferring how I felt about it, to how I felt about everything else! I can't believe I let *him* poison everything in *my* whole world."

"Oh, Sammy boy, you amaze me with your understanding. And you are so, *so* right and sooo, *so* bright! You are going to make a marvelous . . . whatever you decide to go for."

"I didn't make it so great the first time I saw you."

"That time doesn't count. You were hurting so much then that your cognitive ability was off its cogs completely."

"Now that I think back on that black, deep, no daylight, sewage tunnel I wandered through for so long, I'm amazed. I could have gotten out at any time! Nothing held me hostage down there!"

"Yes, something did! Your Neg 'Tudes! By then you had given *them* complete authority, jurisdiction, and prerogative over every aspect of your life, physical, mental, and spiritual, and they were expanding and multiplying and taking over your complete existence like—"

"Like weeds," Sammy interrupted. He was beginning to come out of his deep funk. "I remember Uncle Gordo Gordon once telling me about weeds when I was vacationing on his farm. He'd given me a little plot to grow radishes and a couple of other things that grew fast, so that when Mom and the girls and . . . he . . . came, they'd see what a good farmer I was. Anyway, it was fun till the weeds started to take over. They grew *so* fast, and the other stuff grew so slow, that it took almost all the fun out of gardening. Uncle Gordo kept telling me that life was like that, and that I was getting a great learning experience early that would stand me in good stead. How stupid I was not to have understood that lesson. He and Aunt Marian came out and helped me pull the weeds or I never would have even made it through the project with its sweet returns. Later we all sat on the ground around my garden with a pan of water and washed my spinach and lettuce and radishes and ate them straight out of the ground.

"Why couldn't I have remembered that lesson when I needed it? Why didn't I look for support and reinforcement from *someone*? Probably because I didn't know I could or should then."

"That's too bad, for there are times when all of us, no matter who we are or where we are, need a support system to keep us from getting down below a five-out-of-ten in our lives. All of us should think of someone, while we're feeling good, to whom we could go if something horrific happened to us or even if we had a series of smaller problems, which when added together become a weight too heavy to carry comfortably. I'm sure you can think of someone now."

"Yeah, now I can think of lots of someones: Mom, or (my new principal,) Dr. Davidson, or Mr. Driggs, my school counselor, or Josh, my old tennis teacher, or Uncle Gordo or Aunt Marian or Grandma Gordon, or the preacher at the church where I used to go, if he's still there, or the new preacher if he isn't! Actually I could even call the help line that's advertised on our school bulletin board. I never thought I would before, but any of those things could help nip a problem in the bud couldn't they? Or help a person get turned around?''

"They certainly would help if *you* would let them!''

"Yeah, I'll bet any of them could have and would have helped me see that because one apple on the tree goes rotten, it doesn't mean that none of the rest of the apples are fit to eat.''

"Sammy, you ought to write a book with all your profound sayings in it.''

"Oh yeah, about as likely as my laying eggs.''

"Dare I bring up the fact that you have laid a couple?''

We tried to playfully laugh, and he slapped me on the shoulder. "Leave it to you, my mentor and my confidant, to bring *that* up.''

"I couldn't resist.''

We stopped to stretch, then I said seriously, "I can't understand why it's so hard for people, including myself, to say to someone they trust, 'I am in need of reinforcement *now,* my comfort and self-esteem gauge level is getting close to empty, or please just be there for me till I get things together, or listen to me for a while.' It could be as simple as saying to your mom, 'I need to talk,' or 'I need a hug, a big-long-I-love-you hug, a I'm-glad-you're-part-of-me-and-I'm-part-of-you hug.' ''

"Even the bad part?''

"Cut that out, kid. If you're willing to sell yourself for a nickel, the world will buy you for a nickel. Putting a five-cent price tag on yourself is as foolish and foolhardy as giving a five-cent problem five-hundred-dollars' worth of energy and time. Now, tell me honestly how much *are* you worth?''

''A million? A billion? A zillion? My mom used to read me bedtime stories and tell me I was worth-less''—he laughed—''I mean priceless.''

''Now tell me another good remembrance, and don't you forget it! That is the PRICELESS part!''

''I remember Dorie once hitting me on the head with the telephone and me running over her new Easter hat with my bicycle and Mom having to come out and make us apologize to each other and kiss and make up. But even stuff like that was kind of a goodness and light thing. We wouldn't have *really* hurt each other for anything in the world.''

''Was it after . . . Lance . . . you started *feeding* all the negs in your life, actually encouraging them?''

''Yeah! And I know I did, not just with him, but I started looking for all the faults in everybody else, too.''

''Could we say you stopped altogether trying to make 'sunshine cake' and started putting together only ingredients which make 'cow pies'?''

''You could not only say that, you could say that after the 'Lance thing' *I put into* my life *only* things that made it just one big pile of cow crap.''

''Let's go over that concept one more time. What made the change between the happy times and the miserable times in your life?''

''The ingredients *I put* into it, or allowed others to put into it.''

''Pretend you were making peanut butter cookies and someone dumped in some rat poison by mistake, or on purpose. What would you do?''

''I'd throw out the batter and start over, of course.''

157

"I wonder why we don't do that with mental poisoning?"

"Maybe because the physical stuff is so much more obvious."

"Granted. But isn't one poison as potentially dangerous as the other?"

"Yeah, could be *mental poisoning* is even more dangerous than physical poisoning and maybe self-forgiveness is the equivalent of a second chance."

"You've *put* that thought into your mental computer disk *permanently,* right?"

"Right."

"Now I know this sounds 'elementary, my dear Watson,' but just for the fun of it, let's take turns naming some of the ingredients that instead of making cow pies make one of life's sunshine cakes."

"*Looking* for the good and having a pos 'tude."

"*Doing* the good."

"*Looking* for the kind things."

"Caring how others feel."

"Being in harmony with people and things."

"Wanting to *help* not hurt."

"Knowing that to be happy we have to work at making others happy."

"Loving and allowing yourself to be loved."

"Mostly that! Man, I feel so dumb letting one jerk asshole make me think and act like a complete jerk asshole, too."

"What might have happened if you hadn't *let* him?"

"There's no way I could have stopped him."

"You probably couldn't have kept him from messing up his own life, but might it have been possible for you to have kept your own intact?"

"Well . . . maybe if I'd come to see you then."

"Or maybe talked to your mom, or Mo, or some-one else you care about and trust like you said."

"Maybe? Possibly . . ."

"If you ever have to live through another trau-matic incident, what might you do?"

"For sure, I *wouldn't* allow it to grow until it consumed my life! I'd dump it on somebody! Anybody!"

"Would that be easy?"

"Probably not."

"No one ever said it would be easy."

"Actually, once I got started, dumping the 'Lance thing' was a lot easier than I thought it would be. I'd held that ever-expanding, unspeakable, killer pain and hate for him inside my guts for so long that finally puking it up, even with its nauseating stench and its creeping tissue-disintegrating vileness, was a relief. I feel fifty pounds lighter in weight and a mil-lion times lighter in spirit." Sammy hesitated and quietly sobbed for a long time.

"But I'm still soooo hurting! I'm punctured and bruised and broken and bleeding in every single part of my body and soul. Not only that, but it's like he rubbed salt and broken glass and acid into each of my gaping wounds, rubbed them in while he was laughing and tearing me down in every way known to man. Now the bastard sees I'm beginning to heal, and he won't let me! He doesn't want me to heal! He enjoys seeing me crying and moaning and groan-ing and suffering. He viciously intrudes into my dreams to watch me.

"Sometimes when I'm just sitting in school or maybe having fun, beginning to think I'm maybe get-ting back into a normal life, his gloating face pops up before me, sneering at me, telling me I'm a failure, a misfit nobody that won't . . . *can't* ever make it . . . asking me why I don't just give up and go back to the world of failure where I belong. I see him everywhere. He's always, all the time . . . goading me to . . . you know . . . do it.''

"Whoa, Sammy, slow down. Now could be the time to detach from all your fetid past. Are you ready?''

Sammy shuddered. "I'm ready. At least I think I'm ready.''

"Good. Close your eyes and restfully and slowly take in three big, cleansing, oxygen-filled breaths through your nose, then let go of all the negative toxins in your body as you breathe out through your mouth—cleansing air coming in . . . negative toxins going out!

"Allow your subconscious to say to your material body, 'I see a large, sturdy, white plastic sheet on the floor. I feel quite quiet . . . I feel comfortably relaxed as I start placing all the past negatives of my life in the center of the plastic sheet. IT IS AS THOUGH *SOMEONE ELSE, NOT ME,* IS DOING THE FOLLOWING THINGS.' The detached person hears Lance saying shockingly terrible things about subjects we had always been taught to respect and good things about subjects we had always been taught to disrespect. Don't open your eyes; just see Lance's words and actions as though they were tangible colored blobs being placed in the center of the sheet. What color are they?''

"Red, as red as mixed flames and blood.''

"Next the detached person *sees* the feelings you had when you watched Lance use cocaine. Those tangible blobs are taken and placed on the sheet. What color are they?''

"They're red mixed with black lightning-bolt streaks of shattering electricity."

"Can the detached person see Lance beating up on his son and screaming at him?"

"Yes. It's unreal though."

"What color are those sounds and actions?"

"Black ... hard ... jagged ... some have blood dripping from them and orange-and-green slime."

"What color are the blobs the young innocent boy Sammy sees as he tries to get away?"

"Heavy, heavy, heavy, scared black wiggly lines. Some with scary monster shapes."

"What color are the blobs at the bus station and on the bus, and transferring from one bus to another?"

"Black as the blackest night and piercing like arrows and bullets and axes and knives."

"Have they all been dumped on the pile?"

"Yes."

"What about when the boy Sammy gets home, what colors are there?"

"At first they're almost normal, then blackness begins to filter in from all directions and take over."

"Can those colors be placed on the pile?"

"Yes."

"What color are the hostilities at school?"

"They grow from regular to roadkill pizza colors, to black, deep, sucking-down black."

"Are they dumped?"

"Yes."

"What about the colors during the school gang period?"

"It got to the point where he"—Sammy had begun to say the word *he* for himself—"could only see colors other than black when he was being physically hurt, or road screeching or tagging."

"Can he dump those colors?"

"Yes . . . dumped."

"What about in Las Vegas when Blunt held up the man?"

"Shades of gray and black. Dumped."

"We're in East Los Angeles."

"All black with occasional stabs of red or orange."

"The drive-bys, the hurting young girl who reminded you of Dorie, the dying pregnant girl who had been stabbed?"

"All black with splashes of blood."

"The kitten?"

"The kitten was the only *real* experience there."

"What about being shot and in the Los Angeles General Hospital, the hall, the operating room, being treated disrespectfully, being released?"

"All different shades of black except the long multicolored lines in the halls that even the workers had to use as road maps, the place is so big." Sammy was quiet for a few minutes. "It's all dumped."

"The 'Chicken Hawk' truck driver?"

Sammy took two big, slow, sighing breaths, then the barest smile on his face showed he was thinking of the kind couple in the motor home who had found him at the rest stop. After a minute or two he sighed. "Dumped."

"We forgot to dump the time you hit Mo."

"That was a hurtful black, bleeding black blood from every pore of my body time that I'll never be able to dump."

"You mean you want to carry it around like a sack of bricks for the rest of time?"

"I'm not sure I can do anything else."

"That's up to you."

"Do *you* think I can dump it?"

"I *know* you can if you really want to and you honestly think you should."

"But Mo's the only one I truly love that I actually physically hurt." Sammy had come out of his self-induced trance and opened his eyes wide.

"That's true. But you've got to dump the incident before you can be well enough to repair the damage both to yourself and to her. What good is it going to do to keep on picking and opening up an old wound that needs to be healed? Dump the old, un-clean, toxic, infection-inviting crud and go on to en-courage healthy healing for both her and yourself."

Sammy looked like an innocent five-year-old. "Is it really possible?"

"Yes, It's possible! *If* you wipe the slate clean and start over on building yourself a rewarding, mentally and physically healthy lifestyle."

"I want to! I do want to, more than anything else in the world!"

"Okay, let's do it! Take three big, deep, slow breaths, taking in positives, releasing toxic negatives. Put yourself back into the control state where your actions are subconscious. Feel your thumbs being to-tally relaxed ... your toes totally relaxed ... the muscles in your shoulders and your neck ... totally relaxed, like warm wet noodles. Dump all the rest of your pain and guilt and shame and blame, along with the Mo incident. Can you do that?"

"I guess I can. It's all red and black and green and oozie, and I can smell it. The stench is so bad it's almost strangling me."

"Then relax into an even deeper state and let's pour disinfectant bleach around the edges of the pile. How big is the pile?"

"Big as your La-Z-Boy lounge chair and so ugly it almost has a life of its own. It's moving, almost fighting."

"Of course it's moving and fighting. All those combined negative patternings don't want to leave *you in control of all your emotions and actions*. Let's pour more disinfectant bleach around the whole circle.

"Can you see the bleach begin to disintegrate the negative colors around the edges and in toward the middle of the pile?"

"Yes."

"Is the blob the size of the chair beginning to soften and become smaller as the disinfectant bleach gets to it?"

"Yes. It is. It really is."

We took another fifteen minutes or so to completely disinfect and bleach and disintegrate Sammy's past pain into a white vapor, then into oblivion. "Do you now feel some relief?"

He opened his eyes and smiled. "Only like the world's weight has been lifted off my shoulders. Am I going to feel this good and this light from now on?"

"*Only if* you fill the *vacuum which was left within you* when you took out the dark, hurtful, poisonous negatives, with pleasant, light, healing positives! Don't leave one contagious, toxic thought or concept to multiply and try to take you over again! And be patient with yourself. If at first you don't succeed . . . YOU'RE NORMAL!"

"I can do all that stuff if you'll help me do it!"

"Sorry! I can tell you *how*—the *doing you must do yourself*. But it won't be that hard *if* you make a commitment *TO YOURSELF* to be ever positive, optimistic, compassionate, and long-suffering. Every time you are tempted to say or do or think a negative

164

thing, either bite your tongue or give yourself a good twisting monkey bite on your arm. Some people wear a loose rubber band on their arm and give themselves a good flip.''

"That part sounds doable. And just because Lance is the repulsive, revolting, white trash degenerate jackass of all time doesn't mean that I have to be one too, does it?''

"Absolutely not. In fact, you can be the exact opposite if that's what you want to be.''

"You know, I think the hardest thing was ... to accept what is, as what is.''

"That's often the case.''

"And to know that a person can be a knight in shining armor on the outside and the evilest of demons on the inside. When I was growing up Lance was always Sir Lancelot to me, from the first time I read about King Arthur and the Round table. He was everything good and mighty and bold and honest and honorable. I truly thought that he could save the world, do no wrong, and somewhere in my guts I always felt until *it* happened, that Mom must have done every bit of the stuff that caused the divorce. What a fool I was, an empty-headed blame-the-wrong-person fool.''

"Relax, Sammy. Don't blame yourself or anyone else. Blame, guilt, criticism, condemnation, culpability are all useless, time- and energy-wasting thoughts, verbalizations, or actions. They do nothing to mend, cure, or restore. Teach yourself to fall back on something constructive to yourself and others, instead of destructive. Many of the people I work with feel comfortable working with some form of the Alcoholics Anonymous' Serenity Creed:

"God grant me the serenity to accept the things I

165

cannot change, the courage to change the things I can, and the wisdom to know the difference."

"You told me about that before. It makes complete sense, and honest, I'm trying real hard to keep those thoughts in a place in my brain where I can always pull them out when I need them. I've failed so far, but I am going to keep trying! You were hoping I would say that, weren't you?"

"You are scary. You're reading my mind so often these days."

Then I guess you know I'm thinking maybe I should know some other ways to get rid of the big bad wolves when, like in the fairy story about the three little pigs, one wolf or another is huffing and puffing and trying to blow my house down."

"Well . . . you could learn to *detach yourself.*"

"Like how?"

"Like doctors in medical school have to learn how to '*detach themselves*' so that when they're performing a cesarean section, or doing brain surgery or an amputation—"

Sammy interrupted. "They won't gag or faint when the bloody little baby or the guts pop out, or the little saw buzzes through the skull and the brains hang loose, or the big saw buzzes through the leg, and it drops on the floor—"

I interrupted. "You're a little *overly* graphic, but I'm sure we're both getting *your* picture. Who else can you think of that might have to learn to *detach themselves?*"

"Firemen. I don't see how they can handle carrying out a little kid who is half on fire, or anyone else for that matter, even a dog or a cat. I'm sure they must have some skill in *detaching themselves.*"

"What about policemen?"

"Yeah them too. They must see lots of people shot and stabbed and stuff. And the scary part of it . . . man, I don't know how they do it. Even if they can *detach themselves* some, I'll bet they can't detach completely."

"What about people who work with little babies who are born drug-addicted or grossly deformed, or ambulance drivers, or those of us who work in the mental health field?"

Sammy thought for a few seconds. "I can see by your body language as well as hear from your voice, that you're pained when I'm pained."

"Right, but I can still *detach* myself enough so that if you're going down for the third time, there is no way you can pull me under with you."

"I guess I let Lance do that to me, didn't I?"

"If you think you did."

"Man, life is complicated."

"Not once one makes the choice to be a *Positive Magnet*."

"Bull! That wouldn't, couldn't keep bad things from happening in someone's life."

"You're right. But it isn't what happens in our lives that makes us or breaks us . . ."

"I know. I know. It's what we *do* about what happens."

"Why do you suppose some abused children turn out to be abusers themselves while others don't, or why one generation after another in some families turn out to be on welfare while in others they don't?"

"And some kids whose parents are alcoholics or drug users fall into the same trap and some don't?"

"And some kids brought up in illiterate homes become brilliant educators in numerous fields while others remain illiterate."

"I guess I've tried, even to this very moment, to

shift the responsibility for my totally unacceptable actions onto Lance, haven't I? And it doesn't work that way, does it?"

"Never has, never will."

"Life is geared so that every individual has to *own* and *take responsibility* for every single thing they do, isn't it?"

"With some little leeway for environment, including parenting, etcetera."

"Okay. I think I've got the *Detachment Concept* and the *Responsibility Concept* and the *Positive Magnetic Power Principle* stabilized in my brain. What do I do now?"

"Go home, kid."

"Trying to get rid of me, huh?"

"No. Hold on a minute, I've got some visual aids you should put around in your house, *where you can't ever miss them!*" I brought out three little black bottles with skulls and crossbones on them. Under the crossbones were the words:

DEADLY TOXIC POISONS
NEGATIVITY
PESSIMISM
HOSTILITY

On the other side of the bottles were the words:

DEADLY TOXIC POISONS
HATE, FEAR, DEFEAT
LOW SELF-ESTEEM
BLAME, GUILT

Sammy grinned self-consciously. "Okay, teach. I get the message. See ya when I see ya, and I really am beginning to think *maybe* some day I'll permanently make it out of the dark woods."

"Maybe?"

He poked me in the arm with a single finger. "I'll let you know *that* for sure after our session . . . with you know who."

SUMMARY OF SESSION

Sammy finally faces seeing his father use cocaine. Sammy uses.

His father finds him stoned and having spilled his complete cocaine stash into the heavy carpet, Lance sadistically violently abuses Sammy.

Thursday, September 22

Sammy left the following note in my mail box.

Dear Doctor B:

I stayed awake most of last night rethinking my West Coast nightmare. I can't believe a nice kid like me, from a nice family and home like mine, could ever have sunk so totally into such an insane hellhole. The more sanely I try to disconnect each single incident and go over it in the tiniest possible detail, the more I know now FOR CERTAIN that a lot of the stuff I thought I did do, or did witness, I didn't actually do or personally see! Does that make sense

*to you? Probably not. Well, I'll try to explain.
When I was trashed out on drugs and stuff to
the point where I didn't know which way was
up, I didn't know the difference between movies
and videos and me* watching them *or* being a
part of them. *Like I thought I was part of the
wetback thing, now I* know *I really wasn't because I remember the rest of the movie. It's
weird! Scary black weirder than weird! Anyway, now I'm positively,* absolutely positive I
did not *do some of the stuff I told you I did.*

*I feel sooooo good to know that, and I think
you'll feel good too! It's 3:00* A.M. *and now that
I've delivered this note to you maybe I'll be
able to sleep.*

See ya soon,
Sammy (with all kind of flourishes)

Samuel, Paula, Lance Gordon Family Chart
Saturday, September 24, 2:00 P.M.

Eleventh Visit

Sammy and his mother came early. Sammy sat in his
chair, looking pale, small, and vulnerable, as he
tensely waited for Lance. I had never learned to be
comfortable around child abusers and suspected I
never would, but at least I could be professional, fair,
detached and . . . with a sharp, painful twinge I realized that for Sammy I felt the same mother tiger

170

protective urges that spring forth from all in the female nurturing species. My kid clients *were my kids!* I could detach from them and put their problems in a better perspective than I could with my own offspring, but still I was, and always would be, a protective mother figure fighting for their safety and sanctity!

I had just started a relaxation exercise for the three of us when Lance entered. It was like a cold wind came in with him. I held out my hand. "Hello, I'm Dr. B. Sparks."

The look on his face was that of a wounded animal as he stared soberly at his ex-wife and son. "Paula tells me you've done a lot for Sammy."

"He's done a lot for himself, with a *little* guidance from me. I'm *very* proud of him!"

Lance hung his head. "I'm proud of him, too."

Sammy's body tightened. His face flushed, and he began mumbling things under his breath.

I touched his arm gently. "Relax, Sammy, and *say anything* you are *feeling out loud.* That is the only way we can understand where we're coming from, and how we can get from here to where we want to go."

Sammy tightened his lips until they were just a slash across the bottom of his face. An agonized non-human noise escaped, and tears began to form on his eyelashes.

Lance leaned toward him. "Oh Sammy, Sammy, Sammy, forgive me. Can you ever, ever forgive me?"

Sammy pulled back from him and screamed, "Get the shit away from me, you bastard creep!" He pulled himself into an even tighter little snarl of body parts. "I hate your guts. I hate your liver. I hate your heart. I . . ."

Lance's face turned white as Sammy looked away from him in revulsion. "I deserve that, son. I deserve anything and everything vile you can say."

"You're not fit to be a father . . ."

"I know that only too well . . ."

They both began talking at once. Words bumping into and careening past each other but never getting through. They were both so absorbed in their own worlds of pain.

Paula tried to placate them. "Please, Sammy, don't be so cruel. Your father's hurting, too. And, Lance, you've got to understand how critically . . ." She was simply adding more decibels to the negative, dissonant sound level.

I broke the escalating tension by tinkling a melodic little crystal bell I keep on my desk for such occasions. "I think it is appropriate at this time to introduce the Gordon family to Listening Therapy. We'll put this two-minute sand timer on and take turns talking and listening, if that's all right with each of you."

Sammy shrugged. Paula and Lance, somewhat embarrassed, nodded affirmatively.

"The rules *for LISTENING THERAPY ARE SIMPLE BUT ABSOLUTE!* Let's take turns reading them. Sammy, will you be first?"

SAMMY: When one person is talking, each of the others in the group *must remain silent*. The speaker will have up to two minutes to say what he/she has to say.

PAULA: During the time someone is speaking, the others *must force themselves to listen to what that person is saying!* They *don't have to agree,* but they have to listen.

LANCE: When the speaker has finished, if someone doesn't volunteer, he/she can ask *anyone* in the group to *repeat* what he/she has said.

DR. B: The chosen person does that in *as honest and unbiased a way as possible.*

SAMMY: The original speaker then may try to straighten out discrepancies between what he/she was trying to say and what the hearer thought he/she had said.

PAULA: Others may speak for up to two minutes when they think they can add something constructive without getting off the subject.

DR. B: Only POSITIVE, BUILDING suggestions are allowed. Negative past experiences or thoughts can be brought in only when necessary to *start* restructuring.

SAMMY: Each *questionable* statement made must be followed up by one or two listeners telling what they thought the speaker said.

DR. B: "Listening Therapy is the most reliable method I've found to settle family grievances—in fact, any mode of grievances."

Lance raised his hand. "I'd like to start by telling Sammy how much I love him and how precious he is in my life—"

I interrupted as I looked at Sammy. "I forgot to inform you that according to the Listening Therapy rules, nonverbal expressions are not allowed either.

Listening intently can no more be accomplished with nonverbal talking-back than it can be with verbal interruptions.''

Sammy grinned sheepishly and sat up in his chair.

Lance continued with tears running down his face and onto the front of his shirt. ''I hope someday you can forgive me, dear Sammy, and you too, Paula. I was such a Peter Pan for so many years. I wanted to do what I wanted to do, when I wanted to do it, how I wanted to do it. Something inside me, bigger than I was, nicer than I was, always made me send money, but maybe that was just to salve my conscience.'' He stopped for a couple of seconds, then proceeded.

''I'm going to blurt it all out, every horrendous bit, then if you never want to see or hear from me again I'll understand. I'll ... I'll send you money, but I'll never bother you. I promise, on everything I hold sacred, which is mainly *you*, whether you believe it or not. Anyway, after Sammy and Dana and Dorie were born and I was beginning to climb up the corporate ladder I began to feel ... oh, this hurts ... that I was''—he sniffed—''too good for you''— he sniffed deeply again—''that I was the big shot, the ... how could I have been so stupid? By the time I went to work in Silicon Valley I was as synthetic as it was, and the more successful I became, according to the ways of the world, the more empty and unhappy I was. Then I started drinking and using drugs, just socially, I thought, but after a while I wasn't using them, they were using me! I couldn't understand what was happening in my life. I ...''

The sand ran out of the timer, and I asked Lance who he would like to review what he had said.

He bit his lip. ''Sammy.''

''I heard you say you were the biggest sleazeball

in the world, that you thought you were better than us, too good for us, that you were selfish and self-centered and a dirty rotten, lowest-of-the-low asshole ... sorry, Mom. You said you were plastic and you are. A phony, a wannabe, a rotten dad, a rotten husband, a rotten everything, except a good runner-awayer and a drug addict! The lowest of all, fancy on the outside and on the inside, a disgusting, nauseating, verminous coke-head.''

"Mr. Gordon, would you like to clarify what you really said?" I asked.

"No! He's right. He's absolutely, perfectly, totally right."

"Paula and Sammy, is it all right to give him another two minutes to go on with whatever he has to say?"

Paula was in shock. Sammy was patting and rubbing her hands. They nodded.

Lance continued. "Well, maybe I shouldn't have been so honest, but I had to be, otherwise there is no way in the world Sammy could ever understand my undoing. It was like some subtle evil force was drawing me slowly and painstakingly down into a no-way-out whirlpool. The deeper I got in, the more impossible it was to get out.

"I don't want that kind of thing to happen to Sammy. It's self-destructive, which also means it's destructive to other people, and it can take over so slowly, so subtly, that you're hardly aware that it's become your master. I grew up poor and powerless and some little part of me continued to feel poor and powerless till I started making good money. Then ... I guess the money and the power became my god."

Paula moaned softly. Lance's hand reached out

toward her, then pulled back. He looked at the timer and continued.

"I never stopped loving any of you, though! In fact, I think, the more entangled I became, the more I knew I needed you and wanted you. After each of Sammy's visits, I vowed I would get my life in order, but I didn't when I could have and then ... I couldn't! I remember after Sammy had visited me for two weeks the summer before last, I'd stayed clean and sober for a time, and I was feeling pretty good. I thought I'd licked my problems, and I'd get better and we'd all live happily ever after ..."

The last grain of sand slid from the upper part of the timer. For a couple of seconds the four of us looked at each other in silence, then Lance turned to Sammy. "What did you hear me say that time, son?"

Sammy pulled away and spoke almost to himself. "I heard you say you grew up poor so you were powerless to resist whatever. That's a pile of horse hockey! You were powerless because you're a weak-willed wimp! A Peter Pan who won't grow up and be a man, a decent dad! Mom grew up poor, and she's okay. Poor is no excuse! You have *no* valid, acceptable excuse. You said you loved us. Lies! Friggin' bullshit lies! Black as your heart! Evil as you admit you are! I want outta here. I'm going to throw up. Come on, Mom. We don't need to listen to this crap."

She ran her hand through his hair. "I think we do, Sammy. I really think we do. I'd like to hear the rest of what Lance has to say. At least we should give him that chance, don't you think?"

Sammy muttered, "If it will make *you* feel better, I guess I can wade through a little more of his fly-blown bull-crap lies."

Lance started speaking again. His voice was raspy, and his eyes brimmed with tears. "I deserve that. I deserve everything you've said. I've *been* a deceitful father, a disloyal husband, a despicable human being, but I've changed, believe me I've changed. The night after you ran away, Sammy, I wanted to kill myself, I felt so unworthy, so controlled by all my weaknesses and evil. I almost did it, too, till I remembered that at least you needed me for the money it would take to get you and the girls through college. That was the *only reason* I didn't overdose at that moment, and before I could weaken again I drove to a rehab center and committed myself. They called my company and told them I would be hospitalized for a few weeks. They didn't tell them what kind of hospital it was.

"As soon as I'd dried out a little and felt pretty sure that I'd make it, I started calling you, Sammy, and writing to you, and trying to contact you in every other way I could think of, but you'd shut me out. I wanted back into your lives so much that my fingernails and toenails ached, but I knew I wouldn't ever be able to win back your mother's and the girls' love and respect until I first won back yours. And I couldn't love and respect myself until *you* all loved and respected me. Do you think you ever will be able to do that, Sammy?"

Sammy cringed. "How could I ever, *ever*, EVER respect anyone who abused me, beat me, and cursed me, and"—his words were barely audible—"loved his shit (cocaine) more than he loved me."

"Oh, Sammy, I have never before, and never will, love anything like I love my family. You are the air I breathe, the sunshine that warms my soul, part of

177

the God I worship. Haven't you read any of the letters I've written or the telegrams I've sent?''

''No! I tear them up! Then I toss them in the trash where they belong.''

''What about the letters I sent to Paula?''

Paula replied, ''Like I told you on the phone, Sammy made me promise I'd never mention your name around him.''

''I said I'd disappear again and *never* come back if she did. I'm only suffering through this waste of time now because she pleaded with me to. After all the crap you've put her through, I finally felt I had to do it, but I want you to understand it's just for her! We don't need you in our lives. Why don't you get the hell out? Why didn't you just O.D. when you knew you should?''

Lance's voice was quiet and slow. ''I hear your pain. I know it. It's been a constant companion of mine for many years. Especially when your mom told me what had happened to you. I accept the blame. I should have told her then about my drug addiction, but for some crazy reason I felt I had to explain it to you first. I guess because I knew if you couldn't forgive me, she never could. And there's no way I would ever break you up.''

''As though you could.''

''I know I couldn't, and, honestly, I wouldn't want to, but at least let me tell you the rest.''

Sammy shrugged noncommittally. Paula leaned forward.

''While I was in rehab I accepted, and set out to deal with, my being an addict—a literally imprisoned, completely, mind-and-body–controlled salve to drugs. It's strange how long I'd been in denial. Even when I saw you using my stuff, Sammy, and my heart being smashed to pulp by the anguish and terror that came with the thought of you digging yourself into the dark, irreversible hole that I had dug myself into, I denied it. Those of us who use always know some people who have gone off the deep end, but we keep telling ourselves we aren't like them.

"I think my fear and pain were the things that derailed me when I saw *you* stoned, WITH *MY* STUFF. I felt so responsible, so depraved, so ungodly, such a bad example of a father, such a poor excuse for a human being. Somehow in my nonworking insane mind, it seemed sane that I could force you into submission to the point where you would never want to use drugs again. I could berate you into wanting to be clean and sober, straight and undeviating, for the rest of your life. What an inane fool I was."

"Yeah, what a crazy fool you were, then and now! You didn't know the night before I'd seen you and your out in never-never land buddies acting like the asses you really are."

"Oh, Sammy, I am so sorry! It shows how low I'd sunk to even do it while you were in the house."

"I'll buy that."

"I have no acceptable excuse for my behavior. I just want you to know that that night when I went crazy with you, I honestly thought in my crippled, diseased mind that I was doing what was right. I wasn't stoned, but I felt that yelling and shaking you was the way to stop you from getting into what I had so stupidly embraced."

"Right! You were being sincere and honorable, trying in a most fatherly way to kill me!"

"Sam, I was desperate! I was so far behind with my car payments and my condo payments and my gas and light and credit card payments that I knew I would soon be losing everything. I suspected that even my job was in jeopardy. I sometimes had nightmares of being on the streets begging for just enough to get me a jolt. It was horrible, and yet I couldn't quit . . . I still denied being hooked."

I interrupted since we had gotten to the point where we were no longer using the timer. "Sammy, would you like to repeat what you've heard your father say?"

"No."

"Will you anyway?"

Sammy looked at his mother. She nodded pleadingly. "Okay, only for you," he said. Suddenly he became very sober. "I was trying hard *not* to listen, but I couldn't keep the sharp-arrow words out of my ears and body. He said he was an addict, and he sometimes had nightmares that he'd soon be on skid row panhandling for nickels and dimes and quarters to get enough for a line to keep his body from breaking apart. He said he was afraid he was about to lose his job and he wouldn't have any money to help Mom support us." His next words were almost a whisper. "And he said he went crazy on me because he loved me and because he was so scared he had influenced me to follow in his footsteps."

"How did that make you *feel* Sammy?" I asked him.

"Well, I dunno."

"Do think you might have done something similar UNDER THE SAME CIRCUMSTANCES?"

"I'd *never* have allowed myself to get *there!*"

"I never in my wildest nightmares dreamed I'd get there either," Lance said, "until I was *already there* and couldn't get out! I tried many, many times, sometimes staying clean and sober for up to a month or so. Then I'd think I was okay and that I could just party occasionally ... I couldn't. I'd be bagged and booted back into the great, deep, dark hole again. I even made semi-attempts at suicide a few times when the loneliness and emptiness and darkness got so great they almost overwhelmed me. I really wanted to do it. In fact, sometimes I thought I'd have to do it. That it was the only way out. Once I even got out all my insurance policies and tried to contrive a suicide that wouldn't look like a suicide." He stopped talking and sat breathing heavily and hugging himself as though he felt he were going to fragment.

After a while Sammy quietly asked, "And?"

"I couldn't do it. Paula, it was like you and the kids were somehow reaching out to me and holding me back. Although, I can't imagine *why* after I'd ..."

Sammy supplied, "Dumped us when we no longer fit into the image you were trying to create for yourself." He seemed to be vacillating back and forth between being totally set against his father and being pulled a little toward him. "You kind of make me sick, you know. How could we ever trust you after ... everything you've done to hurt us?"

Lance stood up as though he were going to leave. "I guess maybe you can't."

Paula barred his path. "I'll try to trust you again, Lance. I'll help you if I can. We got through the problems we had when we were first married: financial, physical, and your stepmother, who did everything she could to destroy our faith and commitment to each other. Remember?"

"It wasn't Marnie. Sometimes she was actually a good mother figure to me. It was her drinking, strictly her drinking doing the talking and thinking, when she ..."

Paula put her hand tenderly on Lance's arm as though he were a helpless, hurting little child. "I know. I know. And I also know that I want to help you find yourself and get your life back in order."

Sammy untangled himself and stumbled to his feet. "Then I'm leaving. The hell with both of you! *I can assure you* that if he hasn't got the guts to *do it,* I have! I—"

I interrupted, trying hard to sound gentle but authoritative. "Sammy, a lot of the thinking here is distorted at the moment. Won't you stay and hear everyone out before you make decisions that may not be the same as you would make after everything is on the table and we get things all sorted out? Remember the problems we had getting your jigsaw puzzle pieces put together?"

"Yes, but . . ."

"I knew you would, Sammy. You've come so far in your ability to cope. Your problem-solving skills often really astound me. I . . ."

"I didn't say I would."

I grinned at him. "You didn't say you wouldn't, either. Please stay, *just for me,* if that's the only thing that will keep you here."

"Okay. But don't try to make me a part of this, put-the-blame-on-us, squeezing out of his own consequences crap."

"You can just listen. You don't have to say a word if you don't want to."

"I *won't* want to."

Lance grabbed Paula's hand and held it so tightly she squeaked. "Oh, Paula, I can't believe what I've done to the life of our firstborn, *our* son! I let white-out take over and rule my brain, my reasoning, my actions. Honestly, I hadn't faced the fact . . . hadn't realized that I was really totally addicted until the night I saw my beloved Sammy . . . using. I couldn't bear it then. I can't bear it now. I went crazy because I loved him so much. I couldn't let him waste his life, too. The mental picture of both of us slouched against a wall on skid row, having no goal in life except our next fix, knocked me over the edge. I lost it. I totally lost it, and I'll be forever sorry. Forever, eternally, constantly sorry." He knelt at Sammy's feet, his face stained with tears. "Please, please, son, don't let me be a bad influence in your life. Take after your mother; listen to her counsel. She'll never guide you incorrectly. I'm so, so sorry, and I wish with all my heart that you could forgive me . . . but I understand if you can't. I don't think I'll ever be able to forgive myself."

Sammy's right hand reached out almost in slow motion, seemingly against his will. "I once thought I couldn't forgive myself for what I did to Mo."

Lance looked up at Sammy as though he were the father and asked innocently, pleadingly, "What did you do?"

"I listened to Mom when she said Mo would forgive me, and to Dr. B. Actually I even remember the exact moment and place when I forgave myself."

"Oh, Sammy, I'm so proud of you, and happy for you. Your mom told me a little about your horrendous experiences, which were probably instigated by my neurotic, drug-crazed actions. How could I have done that when I love you so much? *You* are the greatest accomplishment of my life. My hero, my . . . the best part of me."

Sammy slid off his chair and scrunched down on the floor beside his father. "I'm not any of those good things. I'm just a weak, lily-livered, rebellious teenager who tried to blame all of *my* brainless, awful actions on you. Tried to hurt you by hurting myself. How stupid, how nincompoop stupid I was.''

Lance cradled and rocked him. ''What stupid nincompoops we both were, but I *never* stopped loving you!''

''I think that was maybe the worst part. I'd always almost idolized you even when you sometimes nagged me to clean my room and do my chores around the house and stuff. When I saw you weren't perfect, I ... I ...''

''Oh, Sammy, forgive me, forgive me, forgive me.''

''I not only forgive you, Dad ... I, in some crazy way understand. You did what you did that night because ... you loved me.''

The two of them got up and went over to the couch and sat down with Paula. Lance sat between them, and they all three held hands. Between sniffles Sammy said, ''I lied when I called you a child abuser—the brutal, sadistic beating I told everybody you gave me, and the vile cursing out were so exaggerated that I can hardly believe *I made them up,* but I did! I didn't have any black eyes or broke bones or even bruises, other than a bruised ego, and I enlarged that from a molehill to a mountain. I'm the one that needs to ask your pardon, Dad. Please, Dad ...''

The rest of his sentence, if there was one, was smothered in a deep hug from both his parents. Over and over they weepingly assured and reassured him of their great, and forever, unconditional love for him. I excused myself to the women's room so they could have some privacy. However, the recorder remained on.

Telephone Conversation
SAMUEL (SAMMY) GORDON, 15 years old

"Yo, Dr. B. I know you're really busy and all like that but ..."

"But what, favorite friend Sammy?"

"I need to talk to you. I've *got* to talk to you before you meet again with the family."

"Do you feel comfortable talking about ... whatever ... on the phone?"

"Yeah. I guess it would be as humiliating and shameful one way as the other. It's ... it's about ... my dad. I can't believe I told you so many unforgivable things about him. Lies ... lies ... lies all of them."

I interrupted, "Now wait a minute, Sammy, you're being unfair to yourself. I heard him say what he had done to you."

"I deserved it. Every bit of it."

"Whooooa, boy. Don't you think you both were out of control at the time?"

"But I made things sound a million, trillion, zillion times worse than they were. I wanted to hurt him, make you think he ... you know ..."

"Okay. So that maybe wasn't the smartest or the kindest thing you've ever done in your life. Are you going to be condemned forever for it? Isn't there one single way you can think of to smooth out *that* crinkle in your life as you've smoothed out all the others?"

"Well . . . maybe . . . no. . . . What do you think?"

"I not only think, I *know* you can do it by yourself, possibly, probably, you can do it even better by yourself. Then, not only will you have won the battle you will see yourself as the *winner* you are, always were, always will be!"

"What do you think about my making an appointment with Dad as soon as I get off the phone? We could go sit in the beanbag chairs under the bright light in the laundry room and I could deeply and sincerely tell him how I feel now. How does that strike you?"

"It strikes me as being a fantastically wonderful idea if it strikes you the same."

"Do you think I should tell him about . . . the impression I tried to leave with you so you'd hate him as much as I did, or should I just wipe that out of my mental computer? Could you do that, too?"

I closed my eyes and squinted them. "It's done!"

"Man, I can't believe how much better I feel. I thought finding a solution would be pretty near impossible and it wasn't all that difficult. Do you think he'll forgive me?"

"Do *you* think he'll forgive you?"

"I think he already has."

"How are you coming with the forgiving yourself part?"

"Cinchy. Bye. See ya in a couple of hours, minus the garbage."

"What garbage?"

"Hi, Dana and Dorie. I've heard so much about you I almost feel like we've met before."

Dana: "I'll bet it was all bad if it was from my buggy big brother."

"Wrong! It was all good! I suspect that when he's around you he's too embarrassed to tell you how he *really* feels, so he's more comfortable teasing."

"When he came home this last time he treated me and Dorie like we were angles, like we were perfect, like we didn't ever do anything wrong, like we *couldn't* do anything wrong."

Sammy put his hand playfully over her mouth. "Enough already."

Dorie chimed in, "Now he's back to his old self, mainly picking on us and trying to be the boss all the time."

Paula put her finger to her lips. "Shhh, we're trying to impress Dr. Sparks with what a neat, nice, comfortable, healthy, normal, loving family we are."

The kids giggled and assumed nervous, pious positions.

After they had all seated themselves, I asked, "Anyone want to tell me what's been happening in your lives?" They all started talking at once till I tinkled the little crystal bell. "Sammy, want to tell Dana and Dorie what that means?"

"It means we've started playing the Listening Therapy Game."

"Will you tell the girls about the Listening Therapy Game rules?"

"Yeah. As you've seen, this family can't do without them, even when there are only two or three of us playing."

Lance looked at Sammy and grinned widely.

"Whoever is talking gets to talk for two minutes if they want to. That's how long it takes the sand to run from the top half of the glass bottle into the bottom. During that time no one can interrupt, *comprendé?*" Sammy instructed.

"*Sí,*" both girls answered in Spanish.

"Oh, I forgot practically the main thing. Everybody *has to listen* because maybe they'll be chosen to tell what's been said."

Ten-year-old Dorie made a face and said, "Yucky."

Sammy looked at me playfully. "Is yucky a toxic word?"

I shrugged. "For now, why don't we continue with the Listening Game. Paula, would you like to fill us in on how you've seen the last seven days?"

"Well . . . Lance came home with us after our last session, and we had dinner. Then he and the kids talked and played Scrabble, and I Doubt It till long past their bedtimes. Then Lance went back to his hotel, and the kids and I went to bed."

It was obvious Paula was being very cautious about a situation she wasn't completely sure of.

Every part of Dorie's body had been fidgeting since Paula had first started speaking. Something inside her had almost a life of its own. Paula asked, "Can Dorie take the rest of the two minutes?"

"If she wants to."

Dorie's words erupted every which way out of her mouth. "And Sunday morning Dad took us to McDonald's for breakfast. We all love sausage and Egg McMuffins and Mom won't let us have them often, and then we went to Sunday school, and up the canyon to see the leaves, and for a ride on the little old mine train, and we bought Mrs. Field's cookies, and went to lunch, and took the ski lift up to the top of the mountain so we could see the whole wide world below us, and we played we were the Von Trapp family in *The Sound of Music* and ran through the trees, trying to hide out from the bad people, and . . ."

Sammy poked her and turned her face toward the timer. The last few straggly grains of sand were sifting through its narrow middle.

Dana raised her hand timidly. "Who gets to say what they said?"

We all pointed to her.

"Ummm, Mom said how nice and comfy and warm it was to have Dad home again. It was, in a way, like he'd never been away, even though I was little when he left and Dorie was almost a baby."

Dorie: "Was not! I remember Daddy clear as anything, on my sixth birthday taking just the two of us on a *date*, and . . . ooops . . . sorry." She'd remembered the timer.

Dana: "We were like one of the old rerun TV families with everything sort of fairy-tale, they-lived-happily-ever-after-like and everything, just like Mom said. And I think, in a way, she wanted him to stay with us, but she didn't dare ask, and I think he, in a way, wanted to stay, and he didn't dare ask either.

"And Mom said sometimes Daddy played games

191

really dumb on purpose just so he could let us win. Seeing him be silly is almost the most fun part."

I smiled. "It always astounds me how often people hear someone saying things they haven't said at all, sometimes positive, sometimes negative. Dana, are you sure you were repeating just what your mom said?"

She thought for a second. "I think so, yeah."

"Did the rest of you notice how much she added? Things that probably really did happen, or feelings that she had?"

Seriously, Paula, Lance, and Sammy all nodded their heads in the affirmative.

"People think listening is easy. It isn't! We often hear what we *want* to hear. For instance, Sammy, when you were angry with your dad, could you possibly have honestly *thought* you heard him say things that were *much worse than the things he really did say?*"

"I'm absolutely sure of that now!"

"Can anyone else think of other times when that might have happened?"

Dorie asked, "Are we using the timer?"

"No."

Dorie: "Well, when Mom gets mad at me for not cleaning my room or doing my jobs around the house or something, I sometimes feel that she's calling me lazy and dumb and stuff. But then if I go in my room and cry or just think about it, I know she's just trying to get me to do what I should be doing without her having to nag. And I guess it's more like I'm calling myself lazy and stupid because I feel that's what I am."

"Could you be trying to blame her for your problem?"

"Ummm ... yeah, in a way, I guess."

"What might you do the next time something like that happens?"

"Maybe like ... try a little harder to remember exactly what she really did say?"

"Do you think Listening Therapy could help all our lives?"

Everyone answered quietly and thoughtfully with, "Yeah, could be, I'm sure, uh-huh."

"Anyone else got another example?"

Paula began talking softly, almost to herself. "When Sammy was gone, and I was mentally and physically and emotionally and spiritually at my wit's end, there were times when I'd think people were being overly critical or that they were thinking what an incompetent mother I was or something."

"Now that you're mentally and physically and emotionally and spiritually well again, what are you hearing, not only from their verbal but from their nonverbal communication?" I asked.

"Only positive things. Well, *nearly* always positive things."

"Have their communications changed?"

"No."

"What has changed?"

"How I *listen* to what other people are saying, or trying to say, I guess."

"Sometimes do you think it's more important to *listen* to what people *are trying to say* than to what they are actually saying?"

"Oh, yes, especially with children."

"Dorie, if a four-year-old boy was playing in the sandbox and had his castle almost finished when his mom called and insisted that he come in the house 'right now', what do you think that little boy might think his mom was saying?''

''That he was making a stupid sand castle, and it wasn't important, and he wasn't important either?''

''What if his mom took the time to explain that it was getting dark and he could finish his magnificent castle perfectly in the morning and they'd take some pictures of *it*, the greatest structure ever built by man or boy in the history of mankind?''

''I think he'd think he was cool, and he'd probably come in.''

''Do you think what *we* say and *how* we say it, and the way people *listen* to what we say makes a difference?''

A unanimous ''Yes.''

''Would you like to take home a Listening Therapy Game, so you can all, as family members, become more skilled at listening?''

Unanimous ''Yes.''

''Okay, remind me to give some copies to you before you leave, in case I forget. Now just one more little exercise before we go on. Sammy, will you pass out this lined paper, and, Dorie, will you pass out the pencils? I'm going to give you some what-if questions. Remember, you're going to answer them as though you were listening intently to what he/she is TRYING TO SAY instead of what he/she is really saying. REMEMBER, THE QUESTION IS: *WHAT IS THE PERSON TRYING TO SAY?*

1. You come around a corner and practically bump into a dirty, scraggly-looking street kid. He/she groans, 'Get outta my face.' What do you think he/she is really wanting to communicate to someone, anyone?

A. I am lost and lonely.

B. I like being here and who I am.

C. Please help me.

D. I feel good about myself.

2. Mom, Dad, or one of the kids has had a miserable, rotten, all-around terrible, ego-deflating, physically sickening day (which everyone has once in a while). Said person snaps at you when you ask them a question or don't do exactly what they want you to do when they want you to do it. CAN YOU LISTEN TO WHAT THEY *MEAN* instead of what they say?

A. I'm tired and cranky. Please be patient with me for a little while until I get myself straightened out.

B. I like myself when I'm short-tempered like this.

C. Being mean makes me feel better.

D. Blowing off steam like this is healthy.

E. Somebody's been horrid to me so I have the right to pass it on.

3. Someone at your school, office, or wherever is acting uncaring, unaware, and unconcerned. They knock papers off your desk and don't pick them up or apologize. They step on your toes or do other things that annoy or frustrate you. CAN YOU HEAR WHAT THEY ARE NONVERBALLY SAYING? Should you . . .

A. Tell them what a jerk they are being.

B. Gossip with others about them.

C. Ask them if something is wrong.

D. Ignore them.

What would you do if you found his/her family had been in a horrible accident and were all in the hospital in critical condition?

4. What if on the freeway someone screamed at you as he/she zoomed around you into another lane. Would you:

A. Scream back at them and clench your fists as he/she had done, thereby shooting deadly toxins into your own body, telling yourself you had a right to do that since he/she started the problem.

B. Wonder *why* the person was acting so erratically?

C. Compute in your mind the experience *as a negative visual lesson* regarding how foolish *anyone* appears when they are out of control.

Would listening to the still, small, quiet voice within you, instead of the angry voices outside, keep you at peace, keep your blood pressure down, keep you from pumping poisonous toxins into your body?

If you'll go through the rest of the Listening Therapy Game, the What-If Quiz, and the self-evaluation pages together when you get home, and if you listen to this tape again, you probably will find your answers changing, becoming more positive, more thoughtful, more kind and caring, more nourishing and healing," I said.

"Now, Sammy, why don't you share with us how

you feel about your dad reuniting with you and the rest of the family?"

"I feel great. He always was my hero, except when ..." Sammy shrugged. "But that's over." His voice became wet. "I love him. I respect him! And I can't wait till our lives are all going smoothly again, well a little bit upsy-downsy like all lives go. But just having Dad here is ..." He looked embarrassed.

Dorie chimed in, "I'm happy as can be."

Dana looked at Lance quickly, then looked away. "How do we know that ... *it* won't happen again?" She'd been ten when Lance had left.

I gripped her shoulder tightly. "I'm proud of you, Dana. It takes a strong person to ask difficult questions."

Lance stared Dana straight in the eye, then did the same to the other members of his family. Only Paula's eyes wavered, and her gaze fell to the floor. Lance pleaded, "I was weak. I was young. I was stupid. Like the dumb bear, I wanted to see what was on the other side of the mountain. Dana, do you remember that song we used to sing?"

She started singing it softly. One by one the others joined in:

> The bear went over the mountain
> The bear went over the mountain
> The bear went over the mountain
> To see what he could see.
> And all that he could see
> And all that he could see
> Was the other side of the mountain
> The other side of the mountain
> The other side of the mountain
> Was all that he could see.

"I was like that dumb bear. Because I had come from an underprivileged home with an alcoholic step-mother and a pretty heavy-drinking father and had to work even to put myself through high school, let alone college." Lance looked at Paula and choked up. "I could *never* have accomplished that without the help of your wonderful mother. Anyway, I was like that dumb bear—I just had to see what was on the other side of the mountain. I thought I had missed so much. I didn't know that I had *left* so much. Everything that was good and honest and worthwhile was right here in the sacred family circle: the protection, the love, the security, the growth, everything! I didn't see it then, but I see it now! It was like I was blind. Oh, please, please give me another chance."

Sammy and Dorie pushed their chairs close to his. Dana and Paula smiled but held back. Sensing their discomfort I stood up. "You have all come a long way, and I suspect you have many other things you want to talk over and think over carefully. There's no hurry. Take your time. Talk, listen, think, and look at the long-range program."

Dorie, who was squirming and had gone to the bathroom three times during the session and had obviously been ready to leave for some time, added "And go get some ice cream *now!*"

Sammy started picking up copies of the Listening Therapy Game, the *DISTORTED THINKING EVALUATION*, and the What-If Quiz. "Then after dinner, we'll all do our *homework* together! Mom, can Dad come home to dinner?"

Lance: "Paula, why don't I take you all *out* to dinner?"

Paula didn't have a chance to answer, Sammy and Dorie so happily did it for her.

The Listening Therapy Game was introduced. As usual it was startling to find how often family members *thought they heard* something that wasn't said, but that they wanted to hear! Sammy and Dorie have mended the fences between them and their father. Paula and Dana are still cautious. I am optimistic.

Samuel, Paula, Lance, Dana,
Dorie Gordon Family Chart
Saturday, October 15, 3:30 P.M.

Thirteenth Visit

Paula called and said Lance wanted to have another family meeting, part of it with just him and her, part adding Sammy, and the last portion including the girls. Grandma Gordon, Lance's mother, was visiting for the weekend, and she would bring the children at their appointed times.

Lance and Paula came into the office laughing. "You two look happy."

LANCE: "We are. We're making a lot of good changes in our lives."

PAULA: "But there are still some problems."

DR. B: "There will always be problems. But, it is

199

easier to manage big things if you break them down into little pieces, isn't it? Do you have a certain problem, one in particular?''

PAULA: "Yes, Lance and I are unsure about how much we should tell Dana and Dorie about his past.''

DR. B: "Are you considering it from the point of what will be best for the girls?''

LANCE: "I don't want to lie to them, but neither do I want to burden them with the stupidity of what seems like my long-ago indiscretions . . . especially my drug addiction. I'm not sure it would be good for them, especially at their young ages, to know their father was so weak, so easily led, so concerned about peer pressure and about fitting in. I think they need to have a strong father figure now, someone they can look up to and respect. Dana isn't sure she can trust me at this point. How could she ever learn to trust and accept my opinions and guidance if she knew the worst of my past?''

Paula sighed. "The poor little ten-year-old sweetie. Life is very confusing to her. The bad stuff at the elementary school she'll still be going to next year, the filthy language in the halls, the drugs, the drinking and the rapes she hears and reads about. She feels she can talk to me openly because I'm a nurse, but sometimes I almost wish she wouldn't, it's so depressing. Kids today are bombarded on every side by things that give them wrong, unhealthy messages. One day we were talking about a movie she and some friends had seen, and she said, 'Things have gotten so crazy and mixed up between what's right and what's wrong that I've heard this year even Santa

Claus is going to have trouble deciding who's been naughty and who's been nice.' She meant it as a joke, and I laughed, but it about broke my heart, the concept was so true."

Lance reached over and put his arm around Paula's shoulder. She obviously felt his warm compassion and returned hers. It was a big step forward in their positive healing therapy program. He whispered, "Everything will work out all right, Paula. You're a good, strong, well-balanced mother and your kids will learn from you to pull out the weeds."

Paula sighed. "Like Sammy did?"

"You were not in any way responsible for that. I was! And I'm sure it was thoughts of you that kept him from getting in even deeper than he did."

"I don't know . . ."

"Well, I can't be sure about Sammy, but I can be sure about myself, and *YOU* were the one, your love, your goodness, the pain you'd feel, that kept me from . . . taking that last final permanent step."

Paula whispered, "Blowing out your candle?"

"What?"

Paula was so overcome by quiet sobs that she could no longer speak. I explained for her. "Sammy told both Paula and me, 'It's my candle, I can blow it out if I want to.'"

Lance and Paula clung to each other like small, lost children. Lance repeated over and over, "I didn't know . . . I didn't know he'd sunk to . . . to . . . that depth, too."

I interrupted. "But he didn't blow out his candle! That's the good thing. And isn't it wonderful that you can come here and let me be the Hold-It-Together-Figure so you can both allow yourselves to be a little more in touch with your own tender, vulnerable emotions?''

They both nodded, and Lance whispered, ''Poor, poor little Sammy. No one who hasn't gone through it can understand the totally tortured, no-way-out anguish that possesses a person who finds himself in such an unbearable, excruciating place that ... suicide ... seems like the only way out. Poor, poor, dear, dear Sammy. I wonder if his knowing I too have trod that precarious path helped him understand my ... my ... whatever ...'' He stretched out both arms with his palms up in a helpless gesture.

I offered, ''Do you think it might be a *healing* thing for you and Sammy to talk openly about suicide? Every seventeen minutes someone in the United States commits suicide. It's such a big problem that it can't be hidden or placed in the 'not to be talked about' category any longer. I've found that just airing the subject and saying the word out loud helps to bring it into a governable position. Sammy and I have talked a little about what one can do to combat suicidal thoughts. Working with those concepts, the two of you should be able to strongly fortify each other. Perhaps Sammy will also teach you something about the TOXICITY OF NEGATIVITY.''

Lance looked intrigued. ''If that's what I think it is, I'd like it for the whole family, actually the world family.''

''Maybe we should take up the TOXICITY OF NEGATIVITY when the whole family is together. for now let's finish up the drug business, okay?''

''What do you think we should do?''

''You and Paula have talked about it, I'm sure. What did you decide together you should do?''

''I think in the girls' best interest, it should be

by us considered a mistake forgiven and, someday, hopefully, almost forgotten. Perhaps in later years, if it's necessary, we can explain to the girls. I hope I'm not just being macho and self-serving about this. I've tried very hard not to be," Lance said.

"What do you think, Paula?"

"I don't know. I just don't want to make a big mistake that might come back on us and compound everything later."

"Would it make it easier on the girls, or make them happier if you divulged the information? Would it help Sammy or Lance?"

"No."

"Would it make you feel better, or make Lance feel better about himself?"

"No."

"Can you think of any positive, building, happiness- or peace-giving reasons to parade a past drug problem in front of two innocent little girls? Would that help anyone in any way? I'm not answering for you, I'm simply asking how you feel."

"I feel better. I think I just needed to talk it out a little more. Lance and I don't have much time together, just the two of us, no matter how he divides his weekends. Saturday from about eleven to Sunday about four doesn't leave much one-to-one time for any of us."

"How are you doing with the trust factor, Paula? That is, if you want to talk about it."

"Well ... I want to trust Lance's decisions ... and him ... but it's hard. It is really hard."

Lance held her hand tightly. "I know it's hard for you to trust me completely, Paula, after how deeply I've hurt you and the kids, but thank God you are at

203

least giving me a chance to prove to you that I *can* change, *that I have changed!*"

"I am trying. I do want to!" Then she blurted out, "Am I wrong in not letting him stay with us, I . . . I'm so muddled. Am I being selfish, oversensitive, unforgiving?"

"I wish I could answer those questions for you, Paula, but I don't know what feelings and thoughts you have in your mind and heart. I can only say this: you can't be *wrong* if you're doing what you honestly and sincerely think in your heart is *right*."

Lance leaned closer to her. "That feels right to me too, Paula. After the kids go to bed tonight let's stay up and talk until we feel good about the things we've discussed both here and at home . . . your home. I won't push, I promise! I'll go back to the hotel."

Paula: "Thanks, Lance, and I feel good about *not* telling the girls now that we've looked at it from different angles and talked about it."

Lance smiled broadly. "I'm so glad. I'd hate having my hideous mistakes brought out for everybody to gossip about."

Sammy knocked softly on the door, then popped his head in. "Yo, everybody. Been waiting for me?"

Lance and Paula got up, hugged him, and led him in. "Sure we have, Eggbert. All our lives."

As soon as Sammy had sat down, Lance asked him confidentially, "Sammy, how do you feel about telling the girls about my past drug problem?"

Sammy seemed shocked. "Why would anyone in their right mind want to lay that on those little kids? The *National Enquirer* maybe, but no one who cared a bit about decency or healing or anything else positive and good."

Paula put her hand on his cheek. "We certainly wouldn't want to be counted among those kinds of people."

Sammy looked more secure than either of his parents. "I don't think we should ever tell the girls, or Grandma or Uncle Gordo or anybody! *That* problem should be strictly between Lance and God, just as my old problems should be! What good would it do to dig up that garbage and wallow in it again? We gotta choose between being hogs or eagles as Dr. D. once said."

Lance blew his nose loudly. "I'm with you, son. From this moment on I commit to go soaring through the sky forever! My wallowing-in-the-slop days are over! Honest!"

Sammy grinned from ear to ear. "Me too."

Paula smiled gently. "Me three."

"Paula, get one of your scalpels out of your purse and let's each take a blood oath," Lance teased.

Paula put on her mom face, and Lance and Sammy both snickered and straightened up in their chairs. "I guess we'd better get back to being serious about serious things."

Lance turned to Sammy. "Is there anything you need or want to talk about, anything that needs to be aired here in front of a professional mediator?"

"Uh, no. I think between you and Mom and Dr. B and my new principal at school, I can"—he began to talk like a Shakespearean actor—"dissipate *any negative.* In fact with what I've learned, I can quite easily become completely and absolutely perfect perfection."

Lance and Paula jumped on him. "You, perfect? Fat chance. Give me a break."

I interrupted. "Just in case any one of you do need

some support on *anything, anytime,* what are you going to do to get it?''

Sammy said, ''Talk to someone *positive.* Someone who will help me build myself up instead of let me tear myself down.''

''What can happen when you share your problems with someone who is negative?''

''They feed the problems and help you do the same.''

''Even sometimes when they are sympathizing with you, are they actually exaggerating that *one issue* until it seems to take over every other issue in your life?''

''Yeah.''

''Can it sometimes be so subtle that you aren't even aware of it?''

''Ummm, I guess it could be.''

''Should everyone have *locked away* in their mental computer, where it can't be easily wiped out, who they would talk to, where they would go if things got tight, *before* an emergency has a chance to arise?''

''That makes sense to me,'' said Lance.

''Think of a situation that you might already have faced, or one that you might yet face.''

''Well, if anything like the Mo thing happened again,'' Sammy said.

Lance said, ''Or the Sammy thing.''

''What other potentially explosive situations might come into your life?''

''I dunno ... maybe Blunt or one of the other runners ...'' said Sammy.

''With the knowledge you have *now* would you react differently than you would have reacted before?''

''Definitely.''

"Why don't you take turns naming people or places you could turn to if you needed mental or moral support?"

"I could always call Mom or Dad."

"You."

"Sammy."

"Lance."

"Paula."

"Dr. Davidson."

"I could look in the yellow pages under Mental Health."

"Call the operator and ask for a crisis line number."

"Uncle Gordo."

"I could call Mo or Tommy or Marv."

Paula and Lance both named relatives, friends, and church people they trusted.

I interrupted. "We don't want to take up all the girls' time. It's just as important that everybody, young and old alike, has someone to call for help when they need help so desperately that their own minds aren't working clearly. If you've got something stored in your brain so that it *automatically,* by reflex action, kicks in when it's needed, you're pretty much taken care of. Sammy, do you feel you've got your support standbys lined up just as a reliable insurance policy?"

"Yep."

"Lance?"

"Yep."

"Paula?"

"Yep."

"Then you don't have much need for me anymore, do you?"

Lance: "Yes, we do. We need to go over that

TOXICITY OF NEGATIVITY idea you mentioned, with us and the girls. Isn't it time to call them in?"

I nodded. "If you think so."

Sammy hurried to the door.

Dorie scrambled over me to sit by her dad and Sammy. They were like three tail-wagging puppies. Dana pulled her chair as close as possible to Paula's.

"Is there anything you'd like to talk about, Dana, questions you'd like to ask, or things you'd like to say?"

"Ahhhh . . . no."

"Do you feel comfortable with your dad back in the picture?"

She hung her head. "Not completely, but . . ." She looked up and over at Lance. "I want to. I really want to, it's just . . ." She shrugged.

"That's all right, Dana. It's perfectly normal and acceptable for some people to take a little, or even a lot, longer to put broken pieces back together again."

"It's *normal?* Whew, I've been worrying about that since forever."

Lance's love for her was so powerful, it had an almost-physical form. "Next weekend when I come, maybe you and I can have a couple of hours together, just the two of us, so I can let you know how eternally priceless you are, and always have been, to me."

She smiled self-consciously. "I'd like that."

"Anything else?" I asked.

"I guess not."

"What about you, Dorie?"

"I'm happy as Furball when she's purring her loudest."

"I'm happy as when Dread Red Fred is sleeping in my bed, with his head on my pillow, drooling on me," said Sammy.

"Uooooo . . . You're sick," Dorie responded.

Lance ignored them. "Don't you think it would be a good idea to talk to the girls about having some standby resources in case they need to talk or think something out?"

"Absolutely! Would you like to consider family communication skills for a few minutes? They might help."

Positive grunts, yesses, and yeahs.

"Actually, the greater part of communication has to do with *listening,* and we've talked about that some. Sammy, Dana, Dorie, Paula, Lance, have any of you ever made an *appointment* with each other so you could have some uninterrupted time to talk?"

They all shook their heads and looked puzzled.

"Lance, it would be especially good for you to do this with Dana and perhaps even with Paula, for *real* communication is a highly structured technique, yet at the same time as simple as dirt, like most important things are!"

LANCE: "I agree with that, although I'd never thought about it before."

PAULA: "I'm finding that many of the things I've just taken for granted should *not* just be taken for granted."

DORIE: "Like what?"

PAULA: "Like ... well, like ... just plain talking from the heart! It can make us see things in a completely different way. It can be an important *enlightening* process."

SAMMY: (almost as though he were thinking out loud) "Talking from the heart can make you see things as they really are and always have been—

209

instead of how you wanted them to be or doctored them up to be.''

DR. B: "Too often we think people can, or should be able to, read our minds."

PAULA: "For this family I submit a proposition that from this time on, we all do more 'talking from the heart' to each other."

SAMMY: (Raising his hand) "I'll vote for that."
The others followed his example.

DORIE: "And we could use our light therapy room for our heart talking and Listening Room, too, couldn't we?"

DANA: "But we've only got one beanbag chair in there."

LANCE: "Anyone got anything against buying another beanbag chair on the way home?"

DANA: "It's just the laundry room. It's not very big or fancy."

DR. B: "Do important things have to be big and fancy? Can't they sometimes be small and homey and humble?"

DANA: "I suppose, yeah, maybe humble's the most important thing. That's sure what that room is."

DR. B: "How do you kids feel about, on occasion, when needed, having some special, private time with the person of your choice? Maybe you could even put a DO NOT DISTURB card on the door."

LANCE: "I can bring you a new one every week."

DR. B: "It's imperative, on occasion, to pick a time when you can talk without interruption—no phone calls, no knocking on the door, and no jealousy. Solemnly schedule with each other one-half hour or whatever time you think you'll need and treat that commitment seriously.

"There are only three rules in learning skillful communication. Number one is mirroring. Do you know what that means?"

DORIE: "No."

"It means reflecting something *exactly* the way it was said to you."

"I don't get it."

"I saw a mother duck and six little ducklings following her in a straight line across the road. Repeat that as perfectly as you can."

"You saw a duck and her babies crossing a busy road."

"Let's try it again. I saw a mother duck and her six little ducklings following her in a straight line across the road."

"Oh, you mean I should say *exactly* what you said *exactly* like you said it, like a mirror shows exactly. That's not easy."

"No, it's not easy, but it is worth the effort, at school and at work as well as at home, if you really want to communicate. Do you know that one study showed that over eighty percent of the time people didn't absolutely understand what others were trying to say to them? When they tried to mirror back there was a lot of, 'I thought you said,' 'Didn't you mean,' 'It sounded like . . .' et cetera. Have you ever had that happen in your family?"

They all answered affirmatively regarding: schoolwork, time, household or yard jobs, grocery shopping, et cetera.

"Do you understand now that you can't know

what someone else is thinking or feeling unless you can completely mirror, or tune in, *to them?* What did Dorie miss when she repeated what I'd said?"

"That there were six little ducks."

"That they were walking in a straight line behind the mom."

"Dorie said they were crossing a busy road. You didn't say that."

"What if someone is trying to say, 'I'm hurting' or 'I'm lonely' or 'I'm sad,' and they can't get the exact words out?"

Sammy offered quietly, "I think if you were really listening, *really* communicating, you'd get that message nonverbally from their tone of voice or something."

"Wonderful! To really communicate, is it important to hear with a *listening heart* as well as *listening ears?*"

They all agreed.

"Should the listener feel free to say, 'Did I get that right' or 'Did I hear you say,' or 'Did you mean,' thereby allowing the speaker to say yes or no or add other feelings and/or thoughts?"

Dana said, "I'd think they would have to, sometimes."

"Do you do it?"

"I don't think so, but maybe I do. I don't know, but I'm going to try harder to."

"Good for you, Princess. I'm going to try harder to improve my old listening heart, too," said Lance.

Dana looked up at him with adoration and said shyly, "You used to call me Princess Happy Heart when I was little."

The smile he returned to her was tender and bonding. I said, "Now to *acknowledging,* the second part of skillful communication. It doesn't mean that the hearer has to agree, it simply means they should *acknowledge* that they *understand how the person feels*, that *their* message has gotten through. This is *not the time* for lecturing or becoming reactive or defensive! Sammy, what did you *hear me say* about acknowledgment?''

''That . . . I should let the person know that I'm *trying* to see things from his point of view. That the person has a right . . .'' he shrugged.

Dana finished for him. ''That the person has a right to be different. That his little spot on earth is as important as mine even if I don't absolutely agree with . . .'' She looked at Sammy, made a silly face, and shrugged.

I said, ''You guys are so bright you'll have no trouble with the third part of skillful communication. Can you guess what it is?''

No answers.

''It's empathy. That means trying to see things from the speaker's thinking and feeling and acting level. Trying to *feel* what the speaker is *feeling*, then asking if you're getting the picture. *Sincerely* conveying, 'I imagine you feel scared . . . or lonely . . . or misunderstood . . . or angry . . . or frustrated,' or whatever. Caring alone can make the speaker feel better and draw two people closer. One of my favorite truisms is 'PEOPLE MAY NOT REMEMBER WHAT YOU *SAID*, BUT THEY *WILL REMEMBER HOW YOU MADE THEM FEEL!*' It's the first rule for success and friendship.''

''True! True!'' agreed Sammy. ''But back to being empathetic. It can't solve conflicts can it?''

''No, but in most situations, conflict is not the problem. It's how people deal with *a particular con-*

213

flict that gives it either a happy or an unhappy ending. And we shouldn't have to *always* be right, any more than we should have to *always* be the winner. *IF* you won every single conflict or *IF* you were right about every single thing, you would be the loneliest person in the world, for you would be the *only* person in that bracket, right?"

Enthusiastic, unanimous agreement.

The Gordon family practiced the family communication skills until everyone felt comfortable with mirroring, acknowledging, and empathizing.

Sammy summed it up. "I always thought you guys were the strong, no problems, no-pain people, and I was the weak, whoopsy, screwup. Now . . . wow! I know we're all held together by . . ." He threw up his hands in wonder.

Paula reached over and squeezed his knee. "By each other."

One by one they started sharing intimate loving stories about family conflicts and noncommunications: the time the family had left Dorie at church, the time Sammy had taken old Mrs. Markum's fancy birthday cake to Mrs. Miller, the time Dana had gone to the swimming meet on Friday instead of Saturday.

I finally interrupted. "Why don't you save those for the Family Home Nights you said you were going to start having. For now, let me ask if you think we can be deceived about what we *think* we *see* as well as by what we think we hear?"

Dorie laughed. "No. No way! Words can make things seem different, but when you see something, you really see it."

"Let me show you some pictures to discover if you sometimes see things differently from a different angle as well as hear things differently."

Are you being sucked *down* into darkness and pain?
Are you flowing *away* from darkness?

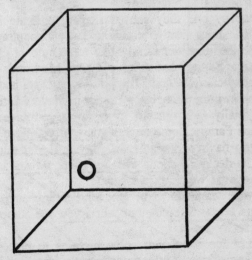

Is *your* circle-self imprisoned inside *your* box or free
on the outside?

The three girls are all the same size. Measure them.
Do you sometimes shrink your self-image?

Are you looking *down* at life?
Are you looking *through* life?
Are you looking *up* at life?

217

Which way is the bird flying?
Have you ever tried to fly both ways at once?

Can you get anywhere if you're flying in circles?

Are you sometimes so busy seeing *things* that you don't see *people*?

Do you see a couple? A vase? Both?

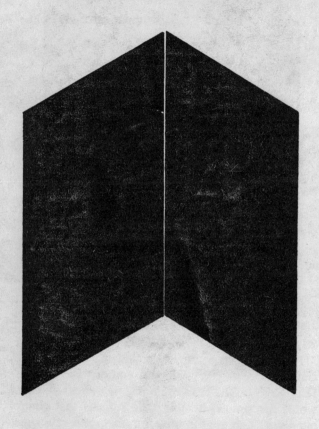

Are you sitting tensely in a dark corner of your dark
little room, looking at another dark corner of your
room?

DANA: "I've really learned some amazing things."

SAMMY: "Me, too. Maybe I'll look at, and listen to, things a little differently now."

DORIE: "I think I'll listen more carefully, and I'll care more."

DANA: "I think I'll *feel* more."

DR. B: "How do you kids *feel* about making appointments to communicate with your parents like you communicate with me?"

DANA: "I can't wait."

DORIE: "I think it will be cool. Just *me* getting all the attention. Having Mom or Dad alone to really listen to me instead of brushing me off because I'm the littlest kid."

"Do any of you have any other things you need or would like to discuss?"

When no one answered, Lance said, "I'd like for you to introduce us to the TOXICITY OF NEGATIVITY."

Dorie made a weird face and looked up at him. "The . . . I don't even know what that means."

I reached into a drawer, pulled out a candy kiss, and tossed it to her. "Oh, yes, you do. The TOXICITY OF NEGATIVITY is just a series of fancy words for simple, humble little truisms that control our lives. You get the prize for *daring* to say something about the show-offishness of the title. Maybe we should find a new one."

Dorie giggled. "No. Let's not. Sometimes it's fun to try and keep your tongue from stumbling when

it's trying to get around words like Tosk sicks ...
tox ticks ... tox sig-a-ne ..."

"Better stop while you've got the candy, kid,"
Sammy warned. "But going back to prizes, how
come I didn't get one or two or three kisses when
... I was 'daring'?"

I pulled out the package. "I think we all deserve
five or ten. The papers will make good visual aids
for our Toco ... tocso ... TOXICITY OF NEGA-
TIVITY Game. Okay, how many of you know that
being negative—thinking negative things, saying
negative things, or doing negative things—can be literally poisonous? Toxic and poisonous mean the
same thing."

Sammy raised his hand and waved it wildly. "I
do, I do, I do, I do!"

"Can negativity be contagious?"

Dorie beamed. "I know! I know! Yes, it can. If
someone says something bad to you, you want to say
something worse back to them."

Dana chimed in. "And if someone comes home
from work kind of crabby, it makes you feel kind of
crabby, too."

"Okay, now that we know negativity can be infec-
tious, let's take turns saying something negative. As
we do so we'll unwrap a kiss and throw the paper
on the floor in the middle of our warm, intimate,
circle. I'll begin, and of course, we'll all have to say
things that other people would say, knowing that
none of us would *ever* be negative or messy in the
slightest way."

Everyone looked embarrassed for a moment, then
began saying negative things and tossing the papers
down.

"I think school is stupid."

"Traffic tie-ups make me want to lash out at people."

"Standing in line drives me crazy."

"The world is full of rude, crude dorks."

"My boss gives me a pain in the neck."

"I despise doing dishes."

"I detest cleaning my room."

"My algebra teacher sometimes makes my head almost explode."

"Most teenagers are stupid jerks."

"I'm a stupid jerk."

"I can't do anything right."

"Nobody likes me."

"I don't like myself."

Dr. B: "Let's take a few seconds to contemplate how saying negative things makes us *look* messy like the floor."

Sammy: "I think saying or even thinking negative things made us *feel* bad, too."

"Physically or mentally?"

"Both, right?"

"The ancient Greek, Roman, Chinese, Indian, and other Eastern civilizations all knew that the body and mind work as one. Later civilization tried to separate them. Now we're again beginning to realize how closely body and mind are connected. What part do you think negativity plays in your mental health or mental illness, Dana?"

"Probably lots."

"Would you like to learn a little game called Ego Aid?"

Dorie started bouncing up and down. "Yes, yes, yes."

"Sammy, will you please set up the card table that is behind that screen? Dorie, will you please take two bottles of pop out of my little refrigerator and put them into this pitcher? Dana, will you please put out a green plastic cup for each of us?''

"Lance and I will pick up the candy wrappers," Paula said.

"I want to be IT if there is an IT," Dorie said.

"We're all going to be ITs. The pop in the pitcher is 'Ego Aid.' When someone says something nice to you they pour about a half inch of 'Ego Aid' into your ego cup. When someone says something bad to you, *you* pour about an inch of *your* 'Ego Aid' back into the pitcher. Got it?''

"May I start?" asked Dana.

"Someone has to."

She looked at Sammy and gulped. "I'm really glad you're home, probably gladder than you'll ever know." She poured some "Ego Aid" into his cup.

Sammy poured "Ego Aid" into everyone's cup. "You're *all* the reasons I had the strength to come back."

Lance poured his "Ego Aid" into the pitcher. "Not I. I drained all the 'Ego Aid' out of your lives . . . and cups."

DR. B: "As we play this game we may sometimes do it for fun, but other times we must do it seriously and be aware of what we have done or are doing to others."

SAMMY: "You did pour a lot of my 'EgoAid' out, but I've got to take responsibility for pouring most of it out myself."

DR. B: "Are you aware that at any one time there are over a *million* kids on the streets? What does that show?"

LANCE: "That 'Ego Aid' isn't being poured as generously as it should be."

PAULA: "And that we've not only got to get it from others, we've got to give plenty of it to ourselves!"

We played the game for about twenty minutes, giving ego trips and breaking down egos. At one time when we were taking turns being negative and hurtful, Sammy's cup was emptied completely. He looked up solemnly. "I'm wondering ... if your ego cup gets emptied often enough and stays empty long enough, could it be terminal?"

Lance and Sammy looked at each other knowingly. The others mulled it over.

Dana seemed unsure. "Being ego-emptied couldn't possibly *kill* someone, I don't think."

Sammy started speaking. He seemed light-years beyond his chronological years. "Draining ego from a person is like adding pebbles, or grains of sand, or small stones, sometimes boulders. They add up in weight or they empty completely until the blackness and heaviness and the imprisoningness of them seem to make living no longer worth the effort."

Dorie's eyes were wide. "I don't believe that."

"Believe it," Sammy said seriously.

"Believe it. Please believe it," Lance echoed.

Dorie looked at me. "Believe it," I said gently.

Dorie grabbed her mom's hand. "That's scary."

"Yes, it's very scary." Sammy, Paula, and Lance agreed.

SAMMY: "Are you going to give us the Ego Aid Game set of instructions to take home?"

DR. B: "Get them off the shelf behind the screen when you put back the card table, okay?"

Paula began stroking Dana's hair. "I'm so grateful we've got our bright-light to sit under and our tapes to listen to ..."

SAMMY: "And our DISTORTED THINKING EVALUATION to fill out ..."

DANA: "And our poison bottles to remind us ..."

PAULA: "And our road maps to mental health or mental illness ..."

LANCE: "And our TOXICITY OF NEGATIVITY Game so we can always be aware of the poisonous effects negative things have on each of our lives."

SAMMY: "Yeah. And now that we've learned that negative things can defile and cripple and weaken and poison and even destroy our bodies and minds, it should make a gigantic positive change in each of our *now* and future attitudes."

LANCE: "Dana, do you see how playing the TOXICITY OF NEGATIVITY Game would make a change in our lives, in your life?"

"Yes. I think it would help me have more self-confidence. In fact from today on, I'm going to start seeing 'negative' as a dark, tearing-down word, and I'm going to start seeing 'positive' as a bright, light, building-up word."

DORIE: I'm going to see 'negative' as an unhappy word and 'positive' as a happy word."

SAMMY: "There's another word I hate that we haven't talked about. It's HATE."

DR. B: "You're right, Sammy. HATE is one of the blackest, most poisonous words of all."

DORIE looked surprised. "But everybody uses it. It's like ... like a nothing word."

DR. B: Are you sure its a 'nothing word'? Can it be a 'nothing word' when it is the exact opposite of the word ..."

Everyone answered, "Love."

Sammy's voice was barely above a whisper. "I remember when I *hated* everything and everybody. It was like a huge black stone around my neck and a spike through my heart; with the most awful of sulfur stenches in my nose and the taste of full-blown rotten eggs in my mouth. As I look back, the scariest thing was that I didn't recognize that all my pain and unforgivable 'acting out' were rooted in HATE. First I *hated* Dad ..."

Lance winced perceptibly.

". . . then I *hated myself.* That hate germinated and then exploded! It sent out longer and longer octopus-type, suction-cupped, tentacles to hold me fast and suck out all the goodness and lovableness from my body and mind as well as my soul."

Lance was hugging Sammy tightly. "But you've conquered that old demon HATE now, son, haven't you?"

"I hope so, because it came so near to sucking the life completely out of me ..."

"I know."

Sammy shuddered. "I think you do, Dad."

DR. B: "We've explored HATE and the negatives

it brings into one's life. Now what say we explore the antidote for HATE?

DORIE: "What's . . . a ant . . . a whatever?"

DR. B: "An antidote is a remedy to counteract a poison, or anything that tends to counteract an evil."

"Oh."

PAULA: "I'm grateful we're trying to find an antidote for HATE. I hear the word thrown around all the time as though it weren't deadly."

SAMMY: "I can't think of an antidote for HATE right now, but I see its color as cold, dark, empty black."

DANA: "And I see Love as pure, clean white, or sunshine-soft summer yellow."

DORIE: "Then maybe LOVE is the antidote to HATE. Could that be?"

DR. B: "Maybe you could experiment and find out."

SAMMY: "Well . . . if HATE is the antithesis—I learned that word in spelling and thought I'd never use it—anyway, if HATE is the exact opposite of LOVE, maybe we could gear up our minds so that when we hear the word HATE, we'll gently and automatically shift into our LOVE mode."

DORIE: "That's super dummm . . . I mean ummm, doable."

DR. B: "Anyone want to give Sammy's theory a try?"

LANCE: "I HATE having to go back to California after being here with all of you."

Sammy snickered. "How are you going to replace *that* with LOVE and still have us all smiling?''

LANCE: "I . . . I . . . LOVE going back to California after being here with all of you because I know each week brings me closer to staying here permanently.''

Everyone clapped and whistled and shouted.

DR. B: "Dorie, do you know that LOVE is a primary emotion?''

DORIE: "I don't even know what you're talking about.''

DR. B: "Sorry . . . that means that *it* was first in time or order of development, the basis or foundation from which all other *good things* derive.''

DORIE: She grinned. "That sounds right, and I believe it because I *feel good when I do good.*''

DR. B: "That's as absolute a reason and proof of the power of goodness and Love as there can possibly be.''

SAMMY: "I second that.''

LANCE: "I third it.''

DORIE: "I fourth it.''

Dana looked at Sammy and started giggling. "I passed it on to you and you ate it.''

They all began laughing uncontrollably. Between snickers, Paula explained, "That's part of an old game we used to play called, There's a Dead Horse on the Hill.''

The laughter was contagious, and I soon joined in.

After we'd simmered down, Sammy asked thoughtfully, "Is it possible always to stay loving and kind and happy?''

"That's not likely,'' I answered, "for life is filled

with both joys and sorrows, ups and down, sunny days and stormy days."

"Sometimes it's too hard."

"That's the precise reason we're learning some skills and techniques to help us through those rocky times."

Sammy took a deep breath and said all in one sentence, "So we'll have the strength-and-mental-computer-locked-in-ability to stop little BOGIES before they become big, black, bone-crushing, over-poweringly monstrous, mind-boggling BOGIES."

We all laughed and clapped. "Yeah for Sammy. Sammy the big, black, boggling, bugger BOGIE bopper."

Everyone tried Sammy's line about the black BOGIE boppers and got their tongues tied up in their teeth. It was fun and refreshing as well as solidifying and healing.

I said, "I hate to bring you all back, but there's one more thing I'd like to add to your mental arsenal: a good understanding of how fear and pain translate into ANGER, which is HATE's twin brother."

Sammy agreed. "I'll buy that. Maybe I should say I'm going to try *not* to buy into either one of *their* programs anymore."

"You've lost me," Dorie and Dana both echoed.

"Okay, lets go back to the lowest denominator: the *first sign* of either HATE or ANGER coming into our lives. Can anyone guess what the precursors, the forerunners of hate and anger would be?" I asked.

No guesses.

"Can any of you see how fear and/or pain could translate or grow into HATE and/or ANGER?"

Sammy folded his arms tightly across his chest

like he was trying to keep something in or trying to keep something out. "I think . . . when Dad and I first had our . . ." (He looked at Dorie.) ". . . disagreement . . . I felt so much pain and fear that I . . . I . . . guess I just let both of them loose to mutate into whatever evil they wanted."

"Ohhh . . . I get it." Dorie nodded. "A few weeks ago I heard that my best friend Sara had said something bad about me, and at first I was hurt, then I dwelt on it until I started some bad gossip about her."

"Did that heal your pain?" I asked Dorie.

"No, it didn't. It made it a hundred times worse."

"So?"

"So then I got mad, at both her and myself, and let my pain grow into ANGER."

Dana looked sad. "Last term Miss Swanson gave me a low grade on one of my papers, and I don't know if I was more pained or scared, but it just got worse until I HATED both her and myself."

Dr. B: "The next time you recognize *fear* or *pain* coming into your lives—*and they will come*—what might you do?

Dana: "I hope I'll remember that *pain* and *fear* can't be kept out of our lives, but HATE and ANGER can; so, I better find some way to let the pain and fear heal normally, like not let it get a terrible infection in it so I could become crippled."

Sammy frowned. "Maybe *truly* crippled mentally! And another thing. It's kind of like there's a stink that goes with HATE and ANGER. It's a . . . like stink that . . . a stink that you can't consciously smell, but it still stinks and after a while nobody in the whole world wants to be around you. Actually you don't even want to be around yourself."

Paula: "I see pain and fear as two little orphan words that are so helpless and vulnerable that the horrible, big, bullies HATE and ANGER will come in and take over their little souls if we let them."

I stood up. "As Sammy says, you're all 'getting your gonzos together,' and by continuing to trust, talk with, and support each other, you're all going to make it to your own promised lands!"

"With each one of our candles burning brightly," Sammy added.

Lance put his arm around his son's shoulders and smiled knowingly. "Yes, precious son, with each one of our candles burning ever so brightly."

SUMMARY OF SESSION
FAMILY SESSION WITH SAMUEL, PAULA,
LANCE, DANA, AND DORIE

It is fantastic and wonderful that the Gordon family now *know* how much they need to, and can, rely on each other! Dear Sammy has traded hostile, unhappiness-causing, depressive negativity in on HAPPINESS-RADIATING AND SUCCESS-INVITING POSITIVITY! His new thinking patterns will ever be worlds away from thoughts of suicide.

Charles Dickens wrote that the 1800s were "the best of times and the worst of times." I think *our time* is the best of times and the worst of times *with the best of kids and the worst of kids!* When I read teenage studies, always in the back of my mind is the wonderment: how many of the hostile, troublemaking, abnormally-acting kids have been brought up in environments which have taught them that that kind of HOSTILE ABNORMAL BEHAVIOR IS NORMAL!

Telephone Conversation
SAMUEL (SAMMY) GORDON, 15 years old

Sammy telephoned.

"Hi, I've got some awesome news. Have you got a minute?' ''

"I've got the rest of my life."

"I know you're busy, so I'll hurry."

"Don't! Just make this a social, not a professional call."

"Are you sure?"

"I'm sure, I'm sure! You're my friend, and I'm as anxious to hear about the good things that are happening to your nice family as you are anxious to tell me. How's Dana doing?"

"She's coming around. I think her trust mechanism is beginning to kick in again."

"Are you the playing the TOXICITY OF NEGATIVITY Game and some of the others?"

"Yeah, and we're listening to our family tapes together and really working at the communication thing. That making appointments to talk to Mom and Dad thing, one to one, in complete privacy, is awesome!"

"I knew you'd like that."

"But let me tell you the best news. Dad's getting a job *here*."

"That's wonderful."

"And guess what else."

"Oh, come on, just tell me."

"Mom and Dad are getting remarried."

"That is, of course, what I hoped would happen."

"Me too."

Sammy hesitated for a couple of seconds. "Actually what I really called to ask you was ... " He hesitated again.

"Hey, it's me. Remember, you can ask *me* anything."

"Well, okay. Mom and Dad are coming home from their honeymoon a week from Sunday, and we wondered if you'd like to come over and help us welcome them back into their new old life. Does that make sense? Anyway, Dorie and Dana and I, and I'm sure Mom and Dad, would like to have you here. Dana and Dorie are making all kinds of cookies and stuff, and Grandma Gordon, who is staying with us while they're gone, is fixing a big turkey."

"Whose idea was all this?"

"Well, sort of mine, but Grandma and Dana and Dorie are doing all the work."

"You're just furnishing the brains?"

"Ha! Together we're making banners and stuff for inside the house and a big WELCOME HOME MR. AND MRS. GORDON sign for over the driveway. It's covered with flowers and music notes and hearts and arrows and stuff, and it's thoroughly awesome."

"Sounds thoroughly awesome."

"And you know what's really the best thing of all?"

"No, but I have a feeling you're going to tell me."

"This is just awesomely awesome. Dana and Dorie and Grandma Gordon have been sneaking around working almost continuously on this big original embroidered motto. They even let me put in a few stitches down in one corner where they wouldn't show. Anyway, it's got hearts and flowers and music notes on it, like the banner, but in the bottom right-hand corner it's got five stupendous candles—five superstupendous, brightly burning candles that no one can ever blow out!''

"I'll bet *that* was your idea, precious Sammy.''

"Yeah, and it's kind of nice to know that you and Mom and Dad and I are the only ones in the whole world who will ever know what those five, forever brightly shining, no-one-can-ever-blow-them-out candles really mean. Maybe someday I'll explain the candles to Dorie and Dana. Do you think I should?''

"I think you should if . . .''

Sammy laughed and finished my sentence, "If I think I should.''

Samuel Gordon Chart
Wednesday, November 23, 12:15 P.M.

Telephone Conversation
SAMUEL (SAMMY) GORDON, 15 years old

The phone rang. It was Sammy. I turned the recorder on. "What's up?''

"I just called to wish you a happy Thanksgiving. I hope you know how thankful I am to you for getting me back on the right track.''

"Thank yourself! I couldn't have gotten you on track if you hadn't wanted to do it.''

"I know you're busy . . .''

"Never too busy for you. I'm just sitting here eating my sack lunch. What's happening in your life?''

"It's beyond stratospheric. Well, most of the time. You know how family and school things are."

"How are you doing with your mind games?"

Sammy's voice became soft and confidential. "It's like something beyond magic has happened to me since I've truly accepted the fact that, like you said, *MY MIND CONTROLS MY BODY, AND I CONTROL MY MIND!* It's almost supernatural or something when I do the hypnotherapy exercises and play the mind games. I feel . . . empowered. I *control* the wonderful and amazing force that is my brain, the power that helps me control not only my thoughts and actions and feelings but helps me influence the thoughts and feelings and actions of others, both positively and negatively. It's a humongous responsibility."

"I'm grateful you now realize *your responsibility in life*, Sammy. I wonder how long it will be before mankind is able to conceptualize a large portion of the brain-actuated control we will eventually have, once we learn more about homing in on it."

"Like what do you mean?"

"Like, what do you know about biofeedback?"

"Well, they hook wires up to your brain and heart and stuff with lots of little pads, to find out what triggers stress and anger and stuff inside you. In time, if you know what thoughts switch on the good energy and what thoughts switch on the bad energy, you can control those mind and body powers.

"Sort of like you can see what's going on inside of you, when you're happy or sad, or mad or glad. Right?"

"I love the panel of little colored lights in front of you that switch on and off so you can see your reactions and how little or big those reactions are."

"I think that's as good and as simple an explanation of biofeedback as I've ever heard. How did you get so smart?"

"Mom showed me a bunch of charts and stuff and the biofeedback machine at the hospital one day when I was there. It's pretty far-out science fiction sort of stuff."

"Yes, biofeedback can *work wonders* for people who will work with it. The amazing machine can even tell your future."

"You're kidding."

"In a sense it can. For instance, if a person allows his/her temper, depression, frustration, or whatever, to raise his/her heart rate and shoot adrenaline into the bloodstream, etcetera, his/her life is in jeopardy of being both physically and mentally compromised or shortened. The machine clearly shows that, doesn't it?"

"Yep! I think everyone should have a biofeedback machine at home. Then we could all solve our problems before we have the problems, keep our little helpless pains and fears from becoming dangerous big ANGERS and HATES."

"Sammy, what I'm going to tell you now really does sound like science fiction. In laboratories around the world, scientists are experimenting with brain-actuated control even as we speak. People have, with brain-actuated control, successfully turned TV and light switches on and off, moved computer cursors and other things, all without touching them. At the Wright-Patterson Air Force Base, people are using their own brain waves to control flight simulators. They can keep their 'plane' on an even keel or dip it from side to side. In a way it is like a video game except that *it is done completely with the mind.*

"The methodology behind the technology is simple and straightforward. Electrodes, similar to those in biofeedback, are attached to the head. They are keyed in to specific brain waves and monitored for voltage changes, which are then interpreted as simple computer commands. For instance, if you wanted to turn on a light, electrodes would be attached to your head in a certain place. At the same time your electroencephalogram (EGG) would graphically show you the voltage of the particular brain wave being monitored. You would think of something that would cause the voltage to increase—some victory, or some fantastic experience that would heighten your senses. That would cause the voltage in the specific brain waves being monitored to rise. When they reach a certain level, the computer would take that as a command to turn on the light and . . . presto . . . the light would turn on.''

"Wow!"

"There is still much research to do in these areas because of the immense complexity of the human brain. Imagine tens of trillions of neurons firing away at any given instant, neurons which are allowing you to weigh options, process concepts, form opinions, learn things, retain information, release it, and telling you when to do what and how to do it. Your brain is sparkling with chemical and electrical activity as well as different types of noises.''

"How many places are working in this area?"

"Many. Grant McMillan, head of the Alternative Control Technology Laboratory works in connection with the rehabilitation of disabled people. Researchers at the New York State Department of Health's Wadsworth Center for Laboratories and Research are concentrating on particular brain patterns known as 'mu rhythms.' They are having success rates ranging from eighty to ninety-five percent.

"Gert Pfurtscheller of the Graz University of Technology in Austria reports that people who have participated in their brain-actuated control studies are totally dumbfounded when they watch their brain waves take control of a computer."

"I would be too! Tell me ..."

I looked at my watch. "Sorry, friend Sammy. It's almost time for my next client friend."

"Do you think you can help him ..."

"Her."

" ... her as much as you helped me?'

"I can if ..."

Sammy finished for me. "I know! ... If she'll *let* you! Good luck."

I needed that. Beautiful little fourteen-year-old Laurie had been abused by her family, then abandoned. The foster parents she had been placed with had also abused her. She deserves to learn about the good things out there that can replace all the bad things that have been shoveled in at her in her past few short years. *Just thinking of Sammy will help me help her!* Maybe sometime I'll tell her about Sammy and his *single lighted candle* that lights up so many worlds, including mine.

EPILOGUE

Almost Lost does not deal with:

Chemical imbalance problems
Deep chronic depression
Bi-polar conditions
Schizophrenia
Hard-core environmentally imposed circumstances
Chronic long-term self-conditioned, internal as well
   as external, hostility, etc.

Such (usually longer-term cases) are referred to
trusted colleagues who specialize in those specific
areas. Many of the above conditions call for prescribed medications.

ALONE

"I felt so alone, so empty. It seemed like being filled with blackness and evil was better than being filled with nothing at all. Life was so painful that it couldn't have been worse if I had been covered with boils from my head to my feet. No one who has not been there can possibly understand."